SEA

Also available in the Target Adventure series:

AWKWARD MAGIC—Elisabeth Beresford
TRAVELLING MAGIC—Elisabeth Beresford

For other Target titles, see end pages of this book

A TARGET ADVENTURE

SEA-GREEN MAGIC

ELISABETH BERESFORD

Illustrated by Ann Tout

a division of

Universal-Tandem Publishing Co., Ltd.,
14 Gloucester Road, London SW7 4RD

First published in Great Britain by Rupert Hart-Davis, Ltd., 1968

First published in this edition by Universal-Tandem Publishing Co., Ltd., 1974

ISBN 0 426 10479 X

Printed in Great Britain by The Anchor Press Ltd., and bound by Wm. Brendon & Son Ltd., both of Tiptree, Essex

Contents

1. The Water Tower Children

THE tide was so far out it looked as if the sea had vanished over the horizon. Johnny slid down the small pebble bank making the stones scatter in all directions and shaded his eyes against the early morning sun. He had never seen the tide as low as this before and he wondered a little anxiously if it would ever come in properly again. Perhaps the sea had gone for good and he would be able to walk all the way from Kent to France. He had never been to France and he imagined that it was full of mountains and quite different from the flat Kent marshes where he lived with his mother and his elder brother and sister.

Johnny screwed up his eyes tightly, but there were no mountain peaks, only the flat wet sands and the humps of small chalky rocks and hundreds of seagulls walking up and down in their funny jerky way.

'Johnny. Johneeeee.'

Johnny hunched his shoulders up to his ears and pretended not to hear his sister's calling voice. There was nowhere to hide so he stood quite still and pretended to be as invisible as the sea.

'There you are, why didn't you answer me?' Lorna scolded, as her small figure appeared at the top of the pebble bank. She rattled down to him, waving a pair of gumboots.

'Go on, put them on,' Lorna said.

Johnny just went on staring across the sands and Lorna, who never could get used to the way he didn't answer if he didn't feel like it, said more crossly still:

'You're wearing your GOOD shoes, and if you get them wet they'll be ruined. Oh you are a trial.'

Johnny pulled off his shoes without bothering to undo the laces and wriggled into his gumboots. They felt rather odd and he stared at them thoughtfully.

'Wrong feet,' said Lorna with a deep sigh. 'Aren't you going to change them?'

Johnny shook his head and started to walk across the sand leaving a line of strange looking footprints behind him.

'Where are you going?' Lorna shouted.

Johnny didn't turn round, he just waved his plastic bucket over his head and Lorna's voice, fainter now, called after him.

'I suppose you're looking for fish. Do be *careful*.'

She would rather have liked to go exploring with him, but there were the beds to be made and the washing up to do so, with another deep sigh, she picked up her brother's shoes and plodded back home.

Johnny walked on, watching with interest the way the sand suddenly went a different colour when he put his weight on it, and then turned to a soft brown jelly when he moved on. There were little ripples in the sand like solid waves and dozens of tiny shells. He picked up a few because Lorna collected them to stick on to boxes to make them into presents. She painted them bright colours and they looked quite nice for a bit, but sometimes they began to smell rather strangely and then the person who had been given a box had to bury it in the dustbin, so that Lorna wouldn't be hurt by seeing her present thrown away.

He came to a thick ridge of seaweed and as he walked through it the tiny sandhoppers went leaping off in all directions. There were worm casts too and crabs so small that when Johnny picked one of them up it was only the size of his little finger-nail. He tipped it back on to the beach and crouched down to watch it burrow into the sand. He was so still that a gull came waddling quite close with its head on one side, its black eyes searching for food.

'Hallo gull,' Johnny said softly.

The gull ruffled up its feathers and then suddenly spread its wings and rose into the sky calling out.

'ha ha ha ha ha.'

And at once all the other gulls round about took to their wings too and began flying round and round shrieking to each other. Johnny looked round and saw a man walking towards him across the sands. He was tall and thin and he was wearing a long overcoat which flapped round his legs. He had his hands clasped behind his back and he was staring at the ground, so he didn't see Johnny until he was almost on top of him. Johnny crouched quite still and looked up at the man who had a pale, beaky face. In fact he was not unlike a gull himself. He seemed rather startled and for a moment neither spoke and then the man made a coughing noise and said.

'Erumph. Looking for crabs?'

Johnny nodded.

'Found any?'

Johnny shook his head.

There was another silence and then the man bent down and looked inside the plastic bucket.

'That's a—a—periwinkle isn't it?'

'It's a *rough* periwinkle,' Johnny said.

'Oh. I see. Well, good morning.'

'Goodbye,' Johnny said politely.

The man ducked his head and marched on and Johnny watched him growing smaller and smaller while the gulls wheeled round overhead and then one by one they landed on the sand and resumed their early morning stroll. Johnny scrambled over the rocks and stopped to watch a prawn darting about in a pool, he tried to catch it in his bucket, but the prawn was far too clever for him and it took refuge under a stone and refused to come out again. There were flat cockles too and limpets clinging fast to the rocks and a velvet crab which was at least six inches across. Johnny had a careful look at the crab's claws and decided to leave it alone, but he did manage to find an empty Great Scallop shell so he took that instead. His mother used the shells for ashtrays in the café.

By standing on tiptoe on top of the largest rock Johnny could just manage to see the curling white edge of the sea and he set out for it as fast as he could go. The gulls all got out of his way, but they didn't bother to fly because he didn't look large enough to be dangerous. He had never been able to explore so far out before and when he came to a whole new ridge of rocks, he found that its pools were full of very strange creatures. There was something which looked like a lobster, except that it didn't have any large claws, just four legs on either side and a pair of long whiskers. Johnny touched one of these whiskers with his finger and the sea animal went scuttling off and disturbed a whole shoal of small fish. They swam backwards and forwards very fast and Johnny put his bucket down into the water, but each time he pulled it up the fish slipped over the side.

'Do keep still,' Johnny said.

But the fish took no notice so he put his hand in and tried to catch one of them that way, but they slid through his fingers. His coat sleeve got very wet and some of the water managed to get inside his gumboots, but it was a very interesting game so he didn't notice. He didn't even look round when a little ripple came surging through the pool making all the seaweed wave backwards and forwards. He thought he had got one fish trapped in a corner, but when he cupped his hand round it the fish suddenly appeared swimming over the top of his thumb.

'Never mind,' said Johnny, 'there's a lovely shell down there.'

He could just see it glinting through the water, a kind of yellowy-brown colour and he got both hands round it and tugged and tugged. But the shell was stuck fast and in the end he had to get down into the pool himself to get a proper grip on it.

'Come ON,' said Johnny and gave a last heave just as a rather bigger ripple came right over his gumboots and made him jump. Perhaps it was the jump that did it, for the shell came loose at last and with a sucking sound it came out of the water and into the sunlight.

It wasn't a shell at all, but a funny, square shaped bottle of very thick glass which had a strange misty look about it. There was a stopper wedged into the neck and there were barnacles and weeds all over it.

'Oy, I say,' shouted a voice.

And Johnny looked up from his treasure and saw what he should have noticed some time ago, that the sea had suddenly decided to return to its usual place further up the beach, and was now doing so very fast indeed. It was all round him and some distance away on the sand was the tall man brandishing his cap and shouting.

'Come on, come on,' the man shouted, waving his arms round and round, 'you'll get cut off.'

Johnny started to scramble over the rocks and then had to go back for his bucket which was bobbing along like a small red boat. His gumboots were so full of water that he could hardly move, so he took them off and clasped them with the bucket and the bottle to his chest, getting a great deal of water all over himself as he did so.

It wasn't easy walking over the rocks in his socks, because the ridges were so sharp they hurt his feet. Obviously the man thought he was taking far too long about it because he suddenly took off his own shoes and socks and rolled up his trouser legs and came wading out to Johnny. He took hold of him by the scruff of his raincoat and bundled him back to the sand with the sea licking at their heels as though it were hungry.

'That was a near thing,' said the man breathlessly. He was quite pale and his hands were shaking as he tried to dry his feet with a handkerchief.

'The tide's turned,' Johnny said helpfully.

'Yes, I did realise that.'

Johnny waited for the man to put on his shoes and socks and then they walked up the beach together until they reached the pebble ridge and then the man said rather sternly:

'You should be more careful. You might have been drowned.'

Johnny didn't say anything and the man sighed in much the same way as Lorna had done and shook his head and went off with his long strides, his hands clasped behind his back. Johnny emptied some more sea water out of his gumboots and tried to put them on again, but they kept getting stuck on his wet socks so he gave up the struggle.

Johnny was very lucky because he didn't live in an ordinary house, but a water tower. Eighty years ago the tower had a large tank on its top floor which had supplied all the water for the cottages round about. But the tank had long since been taken away and because nobody else had much wanted to live in a tower, Johnny's mother had taken it over. It had six rooms one on top of the other. They were very large rooms, although they got smaller as you climbed upwards, and they all had very high ceilings. On the ground floor, which was, of course, the largest of all, there was the kitchen and a tiny bathroom and the café where Johnny's mother served teas and lunches and hot snacks to the holiday visitors. On the first floor was the sitting-room and above that Johnny's mother's bedroom and above that Johnny and above that Lorna and at the very top, Johnny's elder brother Alan.

Johnny pushed open the garden gate and went very quietly up the garden path and even more quietly into the café and he was halfway to the stairs when his mother came out of the kitchen and saw him.

'Johnny!' she said.

Johnny tried to hide the gumboots and the bucket and the bottle behind his back, but he hadn't got rid of all the water and some of it tipped on to the floor.

'Oh, Johnny,' she said again. 'Where *have* you been?'

'Exploring. I brought you a present.'

He took the shell out of the bucket and offered it to her. He had thought of giving her the bottle as well, but even his mother was sometimes not very pleased at some of the things he found on the beach so he kept quiet about it.

'Take off that coat at once. And those socks. Give me your boots. What have you—they're soaking. Lorna!'

'Yes,' Lorna's face appeared over the banisters.

'Take Johnny upstairs and dry him. He probably needs all his clothes changing. Why couldn't you keep an eye on him?'

'There were the beds to make,' Lorna said in an injured voice.

'Oh yes, well never mind. Where's Alan?'

'I don't know,' said Lorna crossing her fingers behind her back.

'Well go on, go on.'

'Don't you want the shell?' Johnny asked.

But his mother had already gone back to the kitchen holding the raincoat and the boots so he put the shell down on the table and climbed the stairs.

'You would,' Lorna grumbled, 'getting me into trouble as well. Did you fall in or something? Your trousers are all wet.'

Johnny shook his head and plodded on up the stairs leaving damp footmarks on each one. Lorna towelled him dry rather roughly because she was cross and he was standing in his underclothes with his hair up in spikes when Alan appeared carrying a notebook and looking worried.

'I think I've got it,' Alan said, sucking at the end of his pencil.

'Got what,' said Lorna dragging a sweater over Johnny's head.

'The way to make some money,' said Alan. 'You could make some sweets and Johnny and I could sell them from door to door.'

'I don't think I make sweets well enough.'

'Yes you do,' Johnny said.

'The last lot melted,' said Lorna, who was now in a very black mood. 'And when I did the toffee, you said it stuck all your teeth together.'

'Yes,' agreed Alan, sucking the place at the back of his mouth where one of his teeth had stuck so firmly to the toffee in question that when he had finally managed to get it out the tooth had come with it. 'Oh well, I'll think of something else.'

They all knew that Money was a Problem. It wasn't too bad in the summer when the visitors came walking and driving across from the marsh road to have meals, but for the rest of the year hardly anybody visited the

Water Tower Café, which was odd because their mother was a very good cook indeed. Lorna always liked it when the café was full and she was allowed to wear an apron and swish about between the tables taking orders and feeling very grand. It was somehow rather sad during the winter seeing it all so empty.

'What have you been doing?' asked Alan, looking at his brother properly for the first time and noticing his ruffled appearance.

'Exploring. The tide was out—as out as—as anything.'

'That's because it's the equinox.'

'What's that?' asked Lorna, who was sure that Alan knew everything.

'It's the time of year, sort of. I wish I'd seen it.'

'I met a man.'

'What man?'

'I don't know. Just a man.'

'You know Mummy doesn't like us talking to strangers,' Lorna said primly.

'We do it all the time in the summer,' said Alan winking at Johnny.

'That's different they're customers.,' Lorna replied.

'Hallo, what've you got there?' asked Alan, picking up the bottle.

'I found it.'

Johnny made a grab for it, but Alan held it out of his reach. It shone dully in the sunlight and all three children stared at it curiously as Alan slowly turned it round and round.

'It's like it's full of mist,' Lorna said.

'It's probably just sea water,' Alan replied, giving the bottle a shake. The mist seemed to get thicker for a moment and then it thinned out again.

'It's mine, it's mine,' said Johnny, struggling into a

clean pair of trousers and trying to get the bottle back at the same time.

'All right, take it easy.'

Alan put the bottle down on the bed and tried to pull out the stopper, but the old limpet shells kept it firmly in place.

'Do be careful,' said Johnny, moving from foot to foot.

'Don't make the bedspread dirty,' Lorna said anxiously.

'I'll use my knife,' said Alan, getting it out of his pocket, 'that should do it.' The limpet shells fell tinkling to the floor one after the other and then with the tip of the blade Alan scraped away the salt and seaweed. 'Got it, it's coming loose,' he said.

'Let me,' Johnny pleaded, 'it *is* my bottle.'

Alan handed it over and with careful fingers Johnny turned the stopper and very slowly, with a faint squeaking sound it suddenly came out.

2. *The Stranger from the Sea*

'THERE, I bet you've broken it,' Alan said.

'No I haven't,' Johnny began and then he shouted, 'oh, oh, oh,' and dropped the bottle as well and sprang backwards against the bed.

'What IS the matter with you?' Alan demanded.

But Johnny only stood still with his mouth wide open and pointed at the bottle which had come to rest against the battered leg of a chair. Alan made a noise like 'tut! tut! tut!' with his tongue against his front teeth which was meant to show Johnny what an idiot he was being, and reached for the bottle and then he too sprang backwards and collided with Lorna.

'Don't touch,' Alan said shakily, catching hold of his sister's arm, 'it's alive.'

'I don't like it, I don't like it, I DON'T LIKE IT,' Lorna said very loudly, 'there's probably an enormous crab or an electric eel inside. Take it AWAY.'

Alan was usually rather brave, but on this occasion instead of doing what Lorna asked he only climbed up on to the bed and dragged her with him. Johnny was there already and the three of them crouched on the creaking springs with their backs pressed to the hard, but reassuring wall and watched the bottle which was now rolling gently from side to side and puffing out little clouds of green smoke.

'What IS it?' said Lorna in a whisper.

Nobody answered so she shut her eyes and put her hands over her ears and began to count up to a hundred in a quick, breathy voice.

'It smells,' said Johnny.

The green smoke was coiling out faster and faster now, spreading across the floor like a thin mist one moment and then jerking in and out at the edges so that it made Johnny think of a sea anemone which is being touched by the returning tide.

'It smells of sherbert,' Alan said, 'and—and curry and seaweed.'

'Thirty-three, thirty-four, thirty-five,' Lorna whispered to herself.

'It's quite a *nice* smell,' Johnny said.

It was, after all, his bottle and no matter what surprising things it chose to do he felt he must stand up for it. The green smoke was twisting itself into a pillar which seemed to grow more and more solid with every second. It was nearly as high as the ceiling and Alan found that he could look right through it and beyond to the pale Spring sky and the wheeling seagulls. And then the smoke suddenly thickened and he was looking into a pair of sad, glass-green eyes.

'Seventy-one, seventy-two, seventy-three,' said Lorna on one side of him.

'It's a person,' said Johnny on the other side.

And it was.

The mist had shrunk and grown rounder and quite solid and standing on the worn carpet was a small, rather surprised looking man wearing very faded trousers, a rumpled shirt and shoes which had once turned up at the toes, but which now lay limply on the floor. Wrapped round his head was what might have been called a turban, but which was now so creased and faded that it looked more like an old scarf. His complexion was green with a touch of yellow and he seemed to be rather out of breath.

'A thousand pardons,' he said, and his voice was soft and lilting and husky at the same time as though he hadn't spoken for a long time.

'Not at all,' said Alan politely.

He was now quite certain that it was all a dream and that at any moment the alarm clock would start ringing and he would hear his mother calling up the stairs. If it *was* a dream then there was nothing of which to be frightened, and in any case the small green person standing in the middle of the round room looked quite harmless and even rather sad.

'Ninety-eight, ninety-nine, a hundred—OH!' said Lorna, opening her eyes, 'who? who? who?' she sounded exactly like a gramaphone record that had got stuck. It was Johnny who went straight to the point by climbing down off the bed and saying with interest.

'You're a genii aren't you? Out of the bottle.'

'Would you mind very much if I corrected that?' the stranger asked.

'Not at all,' said Alan, who like Lorna, seemed to have got stuck with the same words. He banged his elbow against the wall to help himself wake up, but instead of making everything ordinary again, it hurt.

'Not a genii exactly, but a Djinn. With a D you know. There are so many of them and so few of US. You don't mind my mentioning it?'

'Not at...' Alan began and then shook his head violently and climbed down after Johnny and stared very hard at the Djinn who cleared his throat and shifted from foot to foot in embarrassment. 'You mean you're real?' Alan asked cautiously.

'Oh yes, yes indeed.'

'You mean,' said Alan, sticking firmly to the point, 'that you did come out of that bottle?'

The Djinn nodded and bowed and Johnny picked up the bottle and then looked thoughtfully at the Djinn who was only a few inches taller than himself.

'It must have been a bit tight,' Johnny said.

'It was, I assure you.'

There was silence for some moments during which the children went on staring at the Djinn and the Djinn pursed up his pale green mouth and whistled softly and pretended to be very interested in the opposite wall.

'Excuse me,' Lorna said in a small voice.

'Excuse *me* for startling you,' said the Djinn bowing.

'Yes, well,' Lorna twisted her ankles round one another, 'It was a bit strange you know, I mean I've never exactly seen a gen—Djinn before. Excuse me, but have you been in the bottle for long?'

'If, oh Fair Deliverer, you could tell me the date...'

Lorna did so and the Djinn grew even more pale and sallow and counted rapidly on his thin green fingers.

'Four hundred years,' he said, 'four hundred years take or leave a moon or two. Ah my poor master, my poor master.'

'Who's he?' Alan asked.

'A learned Alchemist, young sir.'

'Alche...?' Johnny asked.

'Mist. Physician, magician. One who dabbles in the Mysterious Arts of Science. Do you wish to know more?'

'Yes please,' said Lorna.

They sat down on the edge of the bed and the Djinn sat down cross-legged on the floor and bowed to them. It all seemed very strange to Alan that they should be in Johnny's bedroom with their mother two floors below cooking a perfectly ordinary, although no doubt very nice lunch, while the sea sighed outside and the gulls screamed at each other and at the same time there should be a real Djinn out of a bottle, sitting on the carpet and about to tell them his life story.

'I suppose this *is* really happening?' Alan muttered and Lorna nudged him in the ribs with her sharp elbow so he shook his head again and sat back to listen.

'It all began,' the Djinn said in his soft, gentle voice, 'in Arabia. We Djinns are—were—the servants of the

Mighty Lords and Great Warriors, while the merchants had geniis. There are many of them and very few of us.' He drew himself up and straightened his turban which was slipping over one eye.

'I see. How nice,' said Lorna politely.

'It was,' agreed the Djinn, 'it was also a very great honour to be a Djinn and I was, I admit it, very proud of my position. I was the Personal Slave of a very great Sheik.'

'Sheik?' said Johnny.

'Desert Prince. I was happy in my work. A dust cloud here to confuse his enemies, rubies there to please his—er—friends and so on. Nothing too outstanding of course, but then I was young and only in training. One day there was great excitement in our court for a stranger had arrived and was begging for an audience with my master. I was in attendance behind his throne —I had a new uniform especially for the occasion—when this stranger was brought before us. The trumpets sounded, everybody bowed, even the nightingales in their golden cages were silent. I do hope I'm not boring you?'

'Not at all,' said Alan, 'do go on.'

'The stranger was travel-stained and weary and he spoke with a voice which at first we found hard to understand. But after a rest and some refreshments he told us of many things, marvels of which even we Djinns had never heard, and of lands beyond the desert. He told us of great flashes of fire and a great noise which would bring down the walls of a castle in dust...'

'Gunpowder,' Alan whispered in Johnny's ear.

'And of a glass tube that brought distant sights to one's finger-tips.'

'Telescope,' Johnny said.

'My master listened until the dawn and when the stranger grew weary again he begged him to rest and then to stay with us for ever as our honoured guest. The stranger agreed and every evening as the camp fires were re-kindled we would sit round and he would tell us of more wonders. For a time he was happy, but after many moons he grew restless and began to talk of returning to his own people. My master was a man of understanding and at length he agreed that the stranger should go free. He asked him if there was any gift he would take in payment for all the stories he had told us.'

The Djinn gave an enormous sigh and to the shocked surprise of the boys two large pale green tears slid silently down his cheeks.

'Oh don't,' Lorna said, 'please don't.' She hunted in her pockets and brought out a rather grey handkerchief which she handed to the Djinn. He dried his tears, bowed his thanks and went on more calmly.

'The stranger asked for me. It was, of course, a great honour and I was pleased to go with him, but it was not easy to leave my desert home. Ah, shall I ever again see the camel train dark against the sky at dawn, or hear the soft rustle of the palm trees round a cool oasis or smell the desert as the sun rises?'

'Yes, I'm sure you will,' Alan said firmly, rather afraid that the Djinn was about to start crying again.

'Thank you. But to resume. We travelled many hundreds of miles until we came at last to the sea. It was then that my master unpacked the bottle and asked me to take refuge in it. He did not feel his fellow countrymen would take kindly to seeing me as I then was. You may find it difficult to believe, but in those days I really was rather splendid.'

'You are now, to us,' Lorna said kindly.

The Djinn pulled his faded clothes round himself and gave her a faint smile.

'We reached this country after many months and although I was still heartsick for my own people I was happy. My new master, The Great Horatio, was a good man and he was truly kind, but although all the wonders of which he had spoken were true, his neighbours were very backward in their magic. He had to keep me hidden in my bottle when his friends were in the house. It seems that in your country magic is not an honourable profession?' He looked enquiringly at Alan who said lamely.

'I don't think there's much of it about.'

'Witches?' Lorna suggested helpfully.

'What happened then?' asked Johnny.

The Djinn's face grew even more worried and he began rocking backwards and forwards.

'My master tried to hide from me the fact that his so-called friends were growing to distrust him, even to be afraid of him. They whispered that he was a magician, which was perfectly true, but nothing of which to be ashamed, and one evening some few moons before my time was up...'

'Up?' asked Alan.

'I had been lent to my master for six moons. Only lent, naturally, as no Arabian Prince would ever part with his Djinn for ever. Well my master took me to the sea-shore. I knew he was afraid although he tried to hide it from me. He said that we would meet again shortly and that he was putting the bottle into a secret place among the rocks for just a short time. But I knew, I knew...'

'What happened?' Alan asked as the Djinn paused and sniffed.

'He never returned. Once I thought I caught a glimpse of a mighty fire burning in the darkness, but soon the tide came in and my bottle floated out to sea. Deeper and ever deeper until I was at the bottom of the ocean and there I have remained ever since with only the fish for company. Four hundred years...Ah my poor master. He must be dead by now.'

'Yes I expect so,' Lorna agreed, echoing the Djinn's sigh, 'What a very *sad* story.'

'Your master must have been jolly brave,' Alan said, 'I suppose he knew they were after him—his friends I mean—and he tried to save you. Well I suppose you can go back to Arabia now.'

'I must finish the terms of my agreement first,' the Djinn said, 'after all a contract is a contract even if it's four hundred years old. How grateful I am to you for finding me.'

'It must have been the Equinox,' Alan said thoughtfully, 'it happens twice a year you know and it's when the tide goes out far more than usual. And comes in, too, for that matter.'

'Oh those tides,' the Djinn said shivering, 'backwards and forwards, in and out, up and down. And fish are such very dull company. They never have a thought in their heads beyond where the next meal is coming from. And lobster and crabs, although more intelligent, are usually very bad tempered. And as for the sea urchins, well we all know how *they* got their names.'

'How'll you get back to Arabia?' asked Johnny, who liked to take things one at a time.

The Djinn sank his chin into his hand and stared at the wall, his shoulders bowed.

'Couldn't you sort of magic yourself there?' asked Lorna.

'It's not allowed. You see if we did it would lead to such strange situations. I mean one of us could capture all the diamonds from the South, another could hoard the gold of the West and if one of us was of a warlike character...'

'Yes, I do see that,' Alan agreed.

'Perhaps we could help,' suggested Lorna.

'How?' asked Alan and the Djinn together.

There was a long thoughtful silence which was broken by two things. First by the children's mother, Mrs Craig, calling up the stairs that it was lunchtime and had they washed their hands, and second by Johnny saying,

'Parcel post. Registered.'

'It'd cost a fortune,' Alan said gloomily. They didn't get pocket money in the holidays which meant that nobody ever had any money after the first week.

'Better wash our hands,' Lorna said, getting to her feet. She crossed over to the Djinn and patted his bowed shoulders gently. 'Don't look so sad, Alan'll think of something, he always does. Can I have my handkerchief back please?'

The Djinn scrambled up and gave it to her. It was stained with green right across the middle.

'A thousand apologies,' he said.

'Look here,' Alan said, speaking with his eyes half shut and his forehead creased, signs that he was thinking hard. 'We found you, or at least Johnny did, so doesn't that mean you've got to help *us*?'

'Oh yes indeed,' the Djinn agreed.

'Well supposing we have a bargain. If you do what we want, we'll promise faithfully that you get back to your home.'

'Done,' said the Djinn and put out his thin green hand.

'Children,' said their mother, starting to run up the stairs, 'I've been calling and calling. It's lunchtime. Are you coming or have I got to come and fetch you?'

'Quick,' said Alan, giving the Djinn a push, 'into the cupboard before she sees you.'

'As long as it's not that bottle,' said the Djinn, 'I'll hide anywhere. Four hundred years in one place is more than enough I can assure you.'

And he slid silently into the cupboard and took refuge behind Johnny's best school coat just as the door opened and Mrs Craig came angrily into the room.

3. *The Wicked Landlord*

LUNCH, although delicious—sausage and mash followed by treacle tart—was a rather bad-tempered meal. This was because everybody had something important to think about and it made them all absent-minded.

'Johnny—how MANY times do I have to tell you to brush your hair?' Mrs Craig said.

Johnny hit the top of his head with his hand a couple of times which was his way of being tidy and silently passed his plate for another helping of pudding. The thought of the Djinn not having anything to eat for four hundred years had made him extremely hungry. Lorna, who was sitting next to him, was also thinking about the Djinn, only her mind was on his shabby, crumpled clothes, so she didn't notice the plate until her mother said sharply.

'Wake up, child, for goodness sake. As though I hadn't got enough on my mind without you being so tiresome.'

'What?' asked Alan, wondering for one dreadful moment if his mother knew about their unexpected guest.

'Oh nothing,' Mrs Craig replied, 'nothing that need worry you anyway,' and she smiled in that particularly bright way which made everyone realise that something was very wrong indeed.

'You mean, you know...' began Johnny and Alan interrupted very quickly with.

'Is it the Wicked Landlord, Mum?'

'I wish you wouldn't use that silly name and take your elbows off the table.'

'Yes, but *is* it?'

'Well in a way. Sit up straight.'

Everybody sat up like a ramrod and Mrs Craig looked at their three anxious faces and said more gently.

'It's all right, he isn't going to throw us out into the snow.'

'There isn't any,' said Lorna, glancing out of the window just to make sure.

'It was a joke. Now has everybody finished? Johnny wipe your mouth dear. No—Not with the back of your hand.'

Lorna pulled out her handkerchief and caught hold of one of Johnny's ears before he could twist away and cleaned his face for him.

'You've got that covered in green ink or paint or something,' Mrs Craig said, 'and it's filthy. Really I don't know what you children do with your clothes. Money doesn't grow on trees you know. Give it to me and I'll wash it.'

'I'll do it,' Lorna said quickly, 'and we'll do the washing up too. You go and have a rest.' She was always a little frightened at the back of her mind that when her mother had this funny strained look on her face she might suddenly become ill or faint.

'Well—if you could,' Mrs Craig said hopefully.

'Yes, of course,' said Alan, which was noble of him as he loathed washing up.

'All right then. I think I'll just cycle into Sandstone before—before the shops shut you know.'

They all listened rather apprehensively as their mother went upstairs to put on her coat, but there was no sudden scream or patter of footsteps so they knew that the Djinn was still safe inside Johnny's cupboard. All the same nobody felt quite easy until Mrs Craig came downstairs again and went and got her bicycle out of the shed and pushed it across the garden to the marsh road.

'She's in a bate,' said Johnny.

'Don't talk like that,' Lorna replied sharply, 'it's not

polite and anyway so'd you be in a bate if you had the Wicked Landlord being mean to you, so shut up.'

'Shut up yourself,' said Johnny, whose ear was still tender.

'Shut up both of you,' shouted Alan, which just shows how catching bad temper can be. Lorna put on her mother's apron in a very dignified way and began on the washing up and for a time there was no sound except for the rattle of plates and the slopping of water.

'I wonder if he'd let me wash his clothes for him,' Lorna said at last. She was always the first to give in when there was a row. 'If you lent him some of yours to wear Alan, they should just about fit.'

'OK,' Alan agreed and gave his sister a hefty thump on the shoulder which was his way of saying he was sorry he had shouted at her. Lorna was hanging out the tea-towels and Johnny was staring at the windswept garden and the racing, tumbling grey sea beyond when Alan reappeared with the Djinn behind him.

The Djinn looked even stranger than usual in a pair of faded jeans, a roll-topped sweater and gumboots. He appeared to find them hard to manage and twice he nearly slipped on the stairs.

'I know it's not what you're used to,' Lorna said apologetically, taking the faded green clothes out of the Djinn's hands, 'after all those lovely things you must have had as your uniform.'

'Satins and silks and real peacock's feathers in my turban,' the Djinn said, 'it *was* rather splendid, but still I'm sure these will do very well and it really is most kind of you to take all this trouble.'

He watched with rounded eyes as Lorna turned on the taps and the water came gushing out.

'Could I have your turban as well?' she asked, adding so much detergent that a cloud of bubbles frothed over the sink and slid to the floor. The Djinn's face went a deeper green and he looked so desperately miserable that Lorna wondered if she had said something rude.

'I wonder,' the Djinn whispered to Alan, 'if I might explain to *you*?'

He mumbled against Alan's ear and Alan looked surprised and then thoughtful and then he nodded and went over to the cupboard and got a clean drying up cloth. The Djinn took it and bowed himself out of the kitchen.

'He's not supposed to take his turban off in front of people,' Alan explained, 'apparently it's a Djinn custom. Don't laugh—it's not funny to him.'

The Djinn reappeared wearing the cloth and gave Lorna his turban which he explained proudly was twelve feet long and very difficult to put on correctly.

'Now then,' said Alan as Lorna scrubbed and rubbed in a very professional manner and four hundred years of dust and salt came floating out of the Djinn's clothes, 'now then, about this bargain. You see we've got a Wicked Landlord.'

'Really?' said the Djinn with interest, seating himself cross-legged on the kitchen table, 'so they're still about are they? I *am* surprised. We had a great number of them in my day too. What shall I do with him? Drowning perhaps? Transportation to a distant oasis? Shall all his camels go lame? Or would you prefer something slower?'

'Not anything quite as bad as that,' Alan said hastily, 'but he keeps putting the rent up and we haven't got much money.'

'I was thinking about money,' Johnny said slowly, 'and I was thinking...'

'I wish we could teach him a lesson, that's what,' interrupted Lorna, rinsing away for all she was worth.

The Djinn shut his eyes, put his hands over his ears and bowed his head. He muttered rapidly and then shivered and smiled.

'Done,' he said proudly, 'really I thought I should be entirely out of practice, but then I suppose one never quite loses one's skills.'

'Done,' echoed Alan, 'but I hadn't finished.'

'She wished,' the Djinn explained, 'and I had to obey, it's written into our rules you know. Your Wicked Landlord is now being taught a lesson.'

'But we don't even know who he is!' Alan said.

'Oh that doesn't matter, neither do I,' the Djinn said cheerfully.

'I do,' said Lorna, who had just mopped her hot face with a corner of her apron and in so doing had dropped a letter out of the pocket. She passed it across to the others.

'It's signed A. Blofelt,' said Alan, 'hold on a tick while I read it.'

'Do you think we should?' Lorna asked doubtfully. 'It is Mum's letter.'

Alan had a brief struggle with himself and then nodded. Ever since their father had been killed in an accident two years ago, Alan had considered himself to be the man of the family. If there was going to be more trouble with the Wicked Landlord, then he had better know all about it.

'Yes,' he said.

Everybody read the letter in a different way. The Djinn had the most trouble for he only understood Arabic, so after staring at the typewritten words for a few seconds he gave up. Lorna read it through once and didn't understand it so she went off to hang the laundry on the line. Alan read it through very slowly twice and although he wasn't too clear about some of the words he got the general idea, and Johnny started at the very top of the page and began working his way solidly downwards from the printed heading.

'What's Benovlent?' he asked.

'Benev-o-lent,' said Alan. 'It—it means kind I think, but it's not in the letter.'

'Yes it is. It's the second word. The Benovlent Scottish and Islands Property Company, Ltd. What's Ltd?'

'Limited.'

'Oh. 320 to 323 Grace Street, Edinburgh, Scotland, telephone...'

'You don't have to read all that bit.'

'I do,' said Johnny and started on the date.

'Is it very bad?' asked Lorna, returning from the washing line and admiring her fingers which had gone white and crinkled with being in so much hot water.

'Bad enough,' Alan said gloomily, 'they want to put up the rent again, at least I think they do. Mr Blofelt puts things such a long way round.'

'No wonder Mum was in such a—such a state,' Lorna said, 'still at least the Wicked Landlord's being taught a lesson. Perhaps tomorrow we'll get another letter saying he'll put the rent down.'

Alan and Lorna looked hopefully at the Djinn who

had picked up one of his feet and was carefully examining the sole of his gumboot.

'What's cordially?' asked Johnny, who had got stuck again.

'Friendly. No friendlily.'

'I thought it was lemonade,' said Johnny and started reading the names of the firm's directors down the side of the page.

'Would you like to go for a walk?' Lorna asked the Djinn, feeling that they ought to do something to entertain him.

'If it's what you would like,' the Djinn replied sliding off the table and clumping heavily round the kitchen. Everyone was still rather shy of everyone else except Johnny who shook his head and started at the top of the letter for the second time.

So Alan and Lorna and the Djinn tramped out on to the windy marsh road where the sheep in their thick and rather grey winter fleeces looked at them incuriously. The sea was frothing and hissing right up to the pebble bank and the Djinn glanced at it with acute dislike and pretended to be interested in what Lorna was telling him about the Water Tower. But he had such a lot of trouble keeping his feet and he looked so cold and miserable that Alan soon said, 'Perhaps you'd better go back. But you won't speak to anyone will you?'

'Not if you don't want me to,' said the Djinn looking sadder than ever.

'Now look here,' said Alan as soon as the Djinn was out of earshot. 'We can't possibly keep him with us. Mum'd have a fit if she saw him and it's not only that, supposing we wish something without really meaning it? I could say I wish you'd dry up and you'd probably be dehydrated.'

'What's that?'

'Like those packets of soup which are all little flaky pieces until you put them in water. Mum uses them sometimes.'

'Only if she's in a tearing rush. We couldn't put the poor Djinn back in his bottle, not after he'd been stuck in it for four hundred years,' Lorna said pleadingly. 'Oh, Alan, let's keep him just for a little while. He's so sad and unhappy and we *did* promise we'd get him back to Arabia. Let's ask Miss Pockett at the Post Office how much it'd cost. *Please.*'

'Pounds I bet.'

'Well we don't *know*. He can stay in the tank room, Mum never goes up there. Why,' said Lorna, warming to her theme, 'I expect at this very minute the Wicked Landlord is learning his lesson and everything'll be all right again. You'll see.'

But at that very minute Johnny was saying to the Djinn:

'I've been thinking.'

'Oh yes,' said the Djinn taking off the gumboots and rubbing his pale green toes.

'Mum said that she was going into town before the shops shut,' Johnny went on, 'but it's early closing today so they'd all be shut anyway.'

The Djinn nodded and Johnny looked at him with approval. He liked the Djinn because he didn't keep asking a lot of silly questions or keep trying to tell you things. He didn't boss a person about either. Johnny slid down on to the floor and sat cross-legged too.

'And the other thing,' he said, taking a deep breath,

'was about what mum said about money not growing on trees.'

The Djinn's sad green eyes looked into his with growing interest.

'Supposing,' Johnny said slowly, 'supposing I did a wish...'

4. *The Money Tree*

Mrs Craig came out of the Bank looking even more tired and anxious than she had done before she went in to see the Manager. The Manager had been very kind and friendly, but he had also said quite firmly that he couldn't lend her any more money. The wind had got up and was now sweeping through the main street of Sandstone blowing everything before it, including a great deal of dry, stinging grit. So what with one thing and another, Mrs Craig wasn't really looking where she was going and she walked straight into Mr Antrobus.

It was rather like colliding with a large, but firm balloon for Mr Antrobus was extremely fat.

'There, there,' he said in his deep, wheezing voice, 'and how are you today?'

'Very well thank you,' said Mrs Craig trying to smile politely.

Mr Antrobus, who had known her for a great many years, did not bother to be polite. He stared at her and frowned so that his face went into rubbery wrinkles and his small bright eyes nearly vanished.

'Well you don't look it,' he said, 'in fact you look awful. Come and have a cup of tea with me.'

'No, really,' said Mrs Craig, 'it's very nice of you, but the children are all on their own and...'

'It's not nice of me at all, glad of the company, and as for the children, perfectly capable of looking after themselves. Don't argue.' And he took her arm and led her off down the street before she could say anything more.

Mr Antrobus lived in a very old house which had been altered and added to and knocked about so much that it was one of the sights of Sandstone. The local people didn't know whether to be proud of it or ashamed and in the summer, when the tourists and the holiday makers wandered through the town, most of them stopped to take photographs saying in wondering voices:

'My goodness, did you ever see anything so peculiar?'

Some of the braver—or ruder ones depending on how you look at it—even went so far as to knock on the front door to ask Mr Antrobus if they could come and see round the inside. Mr Antrobus, who hated being disturbed when he was working, would just stand in the doorway without saying a word until the visitor backed away muttering an apology.

'How's your work going?' asked Mrs Craig as her friend opened the door for her.

'Ah, that's the question,' Mr Antrobus replied, 'let us go into the kitchen.'

He squeezed his way through the furniture which was all jammed together and covered with vases, ornaments, books, papers and a great deal of dust. A large black cat whose yellow eyes gleamed like topaz watched them out of the gloom and Mrs Craig almost tripped over a long oak settle which was propped up against the kitchen door.

'Cosy, isn't it?' said Mr Antrobus, looking round contentedly at all the pots, pans and packets which had overflowed on to the floor. 'Now I know I had some tea somewhere.' He began to burrow around like some enormous bear, grunting softly to himself while Mrs Craig cleared a pile of books and two kittens off a chair and sat down.

'Now then,' said Mr Antrobus, when he had found the tea and a kettle and some matches, 'now then, while this thing boils, tell me what's the matter.'

'Nothing, really,' said Mrs Craig, sitting very upright.

'I've known you since you were in your pram, so don't talk nonsense to *me*,' said Mr Antrobus lowering himself on to the creaking settle, and picking up the kittens. 'Come on, out with it.'

'It's, it's the Wicked Landlord,' said Mrs Craig and felt wildly for her handkerchief. 'I just don't see how I can afford to stay on at the Water Tower and we've got nowhere else to go.'

'I say,' said Alan as he and Lorna walked back towards the red brick tower with their heads bent against the wind, 'what's that noise?'

They both stopped and through the thunder of the incoming tide and the bleating of the sheep they could hear something else. A kind of tinkling as though a lot of small bells were being shaken backwards and forwards. They looked round, but there was nothing to be seen except the distant huddle of roofs which was Sandstone and the grass rippling across the marsh.

'It's coming from...' said Alan and stopped.

'It can't be,' said Lorna.

But it was, for there, planted in the middle of the garden which surrounded the water tower, was a tree. It certainly hadn't been there when they left which was odd enough in itself, but even more extraordinary was the fact that it was quite unlike any other tree they had ever seen. It was some twelve feet high with wide, graceful branches and each branch was covered in golden blossom which glinted in the pale afternoon sun. And as the wind shook it the blossom tinkled and clinked as though it were hard and solid instead of soft and frail.

'Well!'

Johnny came rushing out of the tower with the Djinn at his heels. Johnny's face was as round and far more colourful than the sun and even the Djinn looked less seasick than usual.

'Well!' said Johnny again, jumping up and down,

'what do you think of it? Now we don't have to worry about money ever again and I did it. I did it ALL.'

The Djinn coughed delicately behind his pale green hand and Johnny added, 'well it was him really, but I thought of it.'

'What is it?' Alan asked.

'A Money Tree of course. Don't you know a Money Tree when you see one?'

'There aren't such things.'

'Yes, there are,' Johnny said, giving the tree a friendly pat, 'this is one.'

Alan and Lorna went across to it and looked up at the branches with their tinkling burdens of gold coins.

'It's not like any money I've ever seen,' said Lorna, 'money's pound notes and half-crowns and things. This looks like those chocolates you get in your stocking at Christmas.'

'Well it's not, it's real,' argued Johnny.

He had been so pleased with his wonderful idea and now they were spoiling it all for him. He appealed to the Djinn.

'It is real, isn't it?'

'It is to *me*,' the Djinn said cautiously, 'at home—in Arabia that is—when my master's money chests were growing empty we always filled them up with gold pieces such as these. Aren't they what you wanted...' his voice trailed away and Alan, who had been examining the thick gold coins on the lowest branch, said heavily:

'Well we don't have gold money here and anyway this isn't English writing on it, so I'm afraid...'

'It's very *pretty*,' Lorna said.

'But money's money,' Johnny said stubbornly.

'Yes, sort of,' said Alan who couldn't work out the

loophole in this statement although he knew there must be one, 'if you took one of these to the Post Office and tried to buy a sherbert dab with it, I bet the Pocketts wouldn't let you. They'd probably think you'd stolen it or something, see?' And he broke off a gold coin and examined it closely. It was surprisingly heavy.

Johnny's smile vanished and his face puckered up.

'Oh alas and alack,' burst out the Djinn, wringing his hands, 'it's all my fault. I'm a failure. Oh why was I ever made?'

'Oh help,' said Alan, 'I wish, that is, I mean, please don't worry. It's just that you didn't understand properly. I expect your sheik would have been very pleased with a tree like this.'

'Well I thought it was a smashing idea,' said Johnny and began to stamp back towards the Water Tower while Alan, feeling more and more harassed, tried to quieten the wailing Djinn.

'There, there,' he said, pounding him on the shoulder, 'I'm not angry or anything. It's just that we'd better get rid of it before anybody else sees it.'

'You can't un-wish it,' said the Djinn, catching his breath on a sigh, 'at least I can't, because I haven't got that far.'

'You mean we're stuck with it?' Alan asked.

'I expect the holiday makers will like it,' said Lorna, who was still trying to see the bright side of things and who hadn't yet realised, as Alan had, the way people would behave if they discovered a tree covered in 400 year old Arabian gold pieces growing on the edge of the marsh.

'We've got to get rid of it', Alan persisted.

The Djinn gave him a helpless look, his green eyes rolling with distress. Johnny called out.

'There's somebody coming.'

They all became aware of another sound which was rapidly drowning the tinkle of the golden tree. It was a furious barking and yelping mixed with breathless shouts of 'Get down, down I say!'

Everybody turned round and saw a man running across the marsh, his long legs taking him over the rough ground at a shambling trot as he looked back over his shoulder. For biting and snarling at his heels was a very large, black dog. It was frothing at the mouth and it looked so frightening that Lorna shrieked and made a grab for the Djinn, who to judge by his face was equally scared.

'It's him,' said Johnny in astonishment.

'The tree,' said Alan, 'if he sees the tree...'

'Oh the poor man,' whispered Lorna.

'I wish, I wish...' said Alan, looking round frantically, 'I wish the tree was at the bottom of the sea.'

The Djinn drew a deep breath, shut his eyes and muttered and the tinkling stopped and there was nothing to be seen but the windswept marsh and at the same moment Johnny ran forwards and opened the rickety garden gate and shouted:

'In here.'

The man's eyes rolled in their direction and he swerved across the bumpy road and raced through the gate and Johnny slammed it after him just as the dog reached it. The dog yelped furiously and threw itself at the fence.

'It'll get over,' Lorna said, 'oh let's get inside *quickly*.'

They all bundled into the Water Tower and Alan shut the door and leant against it and then four pale white faces and one pale green one appeared at the kitchen window and watched the dog which was still snapping and growling and throwing itself against the fence. The fence, however, had been built to stand up against the great winter gales and it stood fast.

'Thank you,' said the tall man, taking out a handkerchief with a hand which shook violently, 'thank you so much. Really it was all most extraordinary. That brute just appeared out of nowhere and usually you know I get on well with dogs, I really do.'

'I believe you,' said Alan.

'But I've never met one like that before.'

'Nor me,' agreed Lorna.

'It's him,' whispered Johnny, pulling at her sleeve.

'Who?'

'Him. Hallo,' Johnny gave the tall man a beaming smile. The tall man stopped wiping his face and looked puzzled for a moment and then he smiled faintly in return.

'We met this morning on the sand,' Johnny explained, 'we both got wet when the tide came in. Don't you remember?'

'Oh yes, yes of course. Do you mind if I sit down for a moment or two? I feel rather giddy.'

'I'll make you some tea,' said Lorna, 'I expect you'd like that. Grown ups usually do.'

'Thank you, that would be most kind, most kind. Has that animal gone yet?'

'He's going,' said Alan from the window, 'I've never seen a dog like that before. It's got round eyes and its coat's all curly.'

'It's rather like...' said the Djinn and then stopped. The children had forgotten he was there and nobody moved as the stranger said:

'I beg your pardon?'

He looked at the Djinn properly for the first time and his eyebrows rose in surprise for even half hidden by the evening shadows which were stealing across the marsh the Djinn still looked unusual. Both Alan and Lorna tried to think of something to say, but nothing came into their minds and Alan wondered if the tall stranger would suddenly rush out of the Tower and go straight to the police to report that the Craig family were hiding an Arabian Djinn.

'This is my friend Mr Djinn,' said Johnny. 'What's your name?'

'Grant. How-do-you-do Mr—er Chinn is it?'

'Very pleasantly, thank you, sir,' replied the Djinn, nodding and bowing and putting the palms of his hands together. Mr Grant bowed back and then the kettle started to scream in a high-pitched way and the awkward moment was over.

Mr Grant drank his tea very slowly, using both hands to hold his cup because he was still trembling slightly, and the children watched him in silence, hoping that he wasn't going to stay too long because they had to get the Djinn out of sight before their mother returned.

'I haven't been well you see,' said Mr Grant, putting his cup down with great care. 'Overwork the doctor said, so I came down here for some rest and quiet. Oh dear, oh dear.'

'It's all right, the dog's gone now,' said Alan, fidgeting at the window.

'It was all right at first,' Mr Grant went on, his eyes fixed on the kitchen stove as though he were talking more to himself than the children, 'but then this morning your young brother was nearly drowned which gave me quite a shock and then...'

'You never told us about that!' said Lorna, staring at Johnny who stolidly shook his head.

'Am I telling tales?' asked Mr Grant, 'I'm so sorry. And then this afternoon I fell down the stairs at my hotel and when I was walking through Sandstone, the wind nearly blew me right in front of a lorry. Finally I was chased by a wild dog the size of a young calf. It's not very restful is it?'

'No,' agreed Alan, 'but the dog has gone now, honestly.'

'I shouldn't be bothering you with my troubles,' said Mr Grant getting slowly to his feet, 'and you've been most kind. Allow me to pay for the tea.'

'No thank you,' said Alan.

'I didn't mean to be rude,' Mr Grant said hastily, 'but you have got a notice over the door saying Water Tower Café so I thought...'

'That's all right,' said Lorna, feeling sorry for him, 'you see we're really only a café in the summer. We're just us the rest of the time, so you're our friend today.'

'Truly kind,' said Mr Grant in his strange, jerky way. 'One day perhaps I shall be able to do you a good turn.'

He smiled at them, but his eyes still seemed to be looking at something else as though his mind was miles away, until he saw the Djinn's bottle which Lorna had washed and left to dry out on the draining board.

'Good gracious!' Mr Grant exclaimed, 'what a very fine piece. Quite remarkable. Do you mind if I have a look?' He picked it up, turning it gently in his hands. 'Dear me, dear me. At least three hundred years old...'

'Four hundred,' corrected Alan, who had got the door half open by this time.

'Really? Yes, I believe you're right. It's rather scratched of course, but in a remarkable state of preservation otherwise. It's called pebble glass you know because of its thickness. Probably made locally, why it must be almost unique. Does your father collect?'

'Collect what?' asked Johnny.

'He's dead,' said Alan.

'I am sorry,' Mr Grant said, his anxious frown returning, 'I do seem to be putting my foot in it today. Your mother then, does she collect glass?'

'No.'

'Oh,' Mr Grant put the bottle down reluctantly, giving it a final gentle pat. He bowed to everyone again and then looked cautiously out of the door before giving them a final wave and walking rapidly across the garden with his bobbing seagull gait.

'Phew...' said Alan, blowing out his cheeks, 'thank goodness he's gone. He's mad as a hatter if you ask me. Get a move on, Lorna, the washing's still on the line and Djinn, if you don't mind I think you'd better come up to the tank room. Mum'll be back any moment you see.'

'You might have told us that Mr Grant rescued you this morning,' Lorna said to Johnny.

But, like his friend Mr Grant, Johnny's mind was far away and he was staring at the bottle in a way which should have warned the others that he was about to have another brilliant idea.

5. *The Roaring Monster*

KEEPING the Djinn hidden in the Water Tower, was, as everyone soon discovered, rather a worrying business. It wasn't that he was really any trouble, in fact he did his best to keep quiet and out of the way, but as he said to Alan, he would rather not return to his bottle unless it was absolutely necessary.

'After four hundred years in one place,' he said, 'you do get a bit tired of it you know. Of course if it would make it any easier for you...'

'No, no,' protested Alan untruthfully. The Djinn had a way of looking at him with his melancholy green eyes which made Alan afraid he might start crying again.

'We wouldn't dream of it,' put in Lorna, who had come to accept the Djinn in much the same way she would have treated a stray puppy. 'You're all right with us. We'll look after you, won't we Alan?'

'Yes, but...' said Alan, 'oh yes of course.'

He smiled at the Djinn who was playing a very complicated variation of cat's cradle with a piece of string, and pushed Lorna out of the bedroom.

'It's all very well to feel sorry for him,' Alan whispered, 'but it's three days now and we still haven't heard anything from the Wicked Landlord and yesterday the postman nearly walked straight into the Djinn out on the marsh road.'

'He was chasing after a handkerchief which had blown off the line,' Lorna said, 'which reminds me I haven't done his ironing yet. Every time I'm going to start, Mum comes in. It's very awk...oh!'

'Awkward, exactly!' Alan agreed, glad that she was seeing his point of view for once. 'And it's not just that, yesterday the Djinn overheard the milkman saying to Mum that he wished we could have a nice drop of rain to help his runnerbeans along. And you know what happened *then*!'

'It poured,' Lorna said, 'all afternoon. We'll just have to be more careful when there are people about.'

'So you will stay hidden won't you?' Alan said that afternoon to the Djinn, 'Mum wants us to do some shopping for her, so you'll be here on your own. If anyone comes to the door put your hands over your ears.'

'Yes,' the Djinn whispered, 'it's truly not my fault, it's just the way I was made.'

Mrs Craig, unaware of the Djinn playing cat's cradle upstairs, made a very big batch of cakes and set them out on the table to cool and then got the very old vacuum cleaner and hauled it up the stairs to clean the bedrooms. The Djinn, who had just reached a very interesting point in his game, heard the thump of the electric plug as it was dragged along behind the cleaner and dived under Johnny's bed.

'Why can't that boy put anything away,' said Mrs Craig, who—like most people—often talked to herself when she was alone. She began tidying up the mounds of clothes, papers, comics and bits of string which were littered all over the floor and the Djinn watched her feet hurrying backwards and forwards. He had never seen a vacuum cleaner before and he edged a little further out to stare at this odd monster. Mrs Craig plugged it in, pushed the switch and the Djinn's jaw dropped and his eyes bulged as a terrible roar filled the air.

'Oh Great Djinns of the Desert save me,' he implored.

But the Great Djinns took no notice and to the Djinn's horror the roaring, snuffling monster appeared under the bed and came straight towards him with its black, gaping mouth. The Djinn clung to the bed-springs above his head, but the vacuum had seized one end of the piece of string and was now starting to pull it. The other end was firmly wound round the Djinn's wrist and he found himself being slowly drawn towards the cleaner which began to change from a roar to a highpitched whine.

'Drat,' said Mrs Craig, 'it's got caught on something. Oh I do wish Johnny would learn to be more tidy.'

Terrified though he was, the Djinn had to obey and he shut his eyes, muttered and shivered and then as quickly as possible he began to shrink and dissolve, but he wasn't fast enough and with a last triumphant scream the vacuum seized hold of him and sucked him into its greedy mouth.

'Help,' cried the Djinn and then he was turning over and over and whirling up into a dusty darkness that was full of tiny flying objects which circled round his trembling form like furious buzzing insects.

'There,' said Mrs Craig, switching off and moving the bed away from the wall, 'just as I thought. Alan's sweater and his jeans—I was wondering where they'd got to, and his gumboots. What will those children do next? It really is too bad of them.'

She gave the clothes an angry shake, pushed the bed back against the wall and unplugged the cleaner. The Djinn, clinging to the inside of the dust bag, gave himself up for lost as he was carried from room to room and the bag grew fuller and fuller. Even life in a bottle under the sea was preferable to this and he felt thoroughly battered and exhausted when at last Mrs Craig finished the cleaning and carried the vacuum downstairs to the kitchen. She was about to empty it when there was the sound of footsteps followed by a knock on the door.

'Botheration take it,' said Mrs Craig, giving her hair an anxious pat in front of mirror. 'Now who can that be?'

Standing on the step was a very tall, thin man with a black patch over one eye.

'We're closed,' said Mrs Craig rather crossly.

'Oh no really, it's not that. Excuse me but are you the mother of the three children who live here?'

'There's nothing the matter is there? They haven't been in an accident?' asked Mrs Craig, going quite pale.

'No, no, no, nothing of that nature. I'm the one has the accidents,' and he laughed mournfully. 'Only this morning I walked straight into a door. Ridiculous, isn't it?' and he touched the patch over his eye. 'No, as a matter of fact I came to see them about a bottle. My name's Grant by the way, Alexander Grant.'

'A bottle?' echoed Mrs Craig, 'I'm afraid I don't quite understand. But won't you come in?'

Mr Grant tripped over the step and Mrs Craig took him firmly by the arm and led him over to a chair. With many stops and starts he managed to tell her about the dog and his first visit to the Water Tower. He even, to the shivering Djinn's distress, mentioned a Mr Chinn.

'A rather, well, pale little man,' said Mr Grant, 'actually he was pale green.'

'Are you sure,' said Mrs Craig, doubtfully, 'that you're feeling all right?'

'No,' said Mr Grant, passing an even more shaky hand than usual across his forehead, 'I don't believe I am. But I do assure you that he *was* green. However that's beside the point. What I wanted to enquire was, whether that bottle was for sale?'

'What bottle?'

Mr Grant didn't look like a dangerous character, but he certainly behaved in a very odd way.

'The four hundred year old pebble glass bottle. Quite a rarity of its kind. In fact I've never seen one like it before. I should be most happy to give you a good price for it.'

'If I knew anything about this bottle I'd be more than pleased to sell it to you,' said Mrs Craig with a sigh, 'but unfortunately I don't.'

'Oh well, in that case,' said Mr Grant getting to his feet then he noticed Mrs Craig's careworn expression and, because in spite of his own troubles he was a very kindly man, he added. 'Is anything the matter? Is there something I might do to help?'

'No, no,' protested Mrs Craig, who always felt worse when people were nice to her, 'It's nothing, really.'

'I wish I could be of some assistance after the way your children helped me,' said Mr Grant.

The vacuum cleaner quivered a little and the bag rose gently as though a puff of wind had touched it.

'And now if you'll excuse me,' began Mrs Craig when Mr Grant suddenly pointed to the cakes.

'Did you make those?' he asked.

'Yes, but...'

'Splendid,' said Mr Grant, rubbing his long fingers together, 'I've just had an excellent idea. If you're not too busy I wonder if you could make some cakes for me?'

'For *you*!'

'Well not me exactly. I was having a word this morning with your local vicar–stupidly I'd stepped out into the road right in front of a farm tractor and he pulled me out of the way–and he was telling me about the Bring and Buy Sale at the church hall. I should like to make a contribution and it suddenly occurred to me that if you could bake shall we say five–no six–dozen of those little currant things they might be very acceptable. Perhaps a large iced cake as well.'

'Well of course I could,' said Mrs Craig, feeling even more bewildered.

'Would ten pounds cover the cost of the cooking things and your time?' asked Mr Grant feeling for his wallet.

'More than cover it. I don't want charity,' said Mrs Craig going alarmingly straightbacked and looking very much as Alan had done.

'Charity, away with you,' said Mr Grant counting out the notes, 'nothing of the sort. I'd call it a very good business arrangement. After all your children probably saved my life when I was chased by that dog. It was quite mad you know. Now then, do you agree?'

He sounded so brisk and businesslike that Mrs Craig nodded and Mr Grant counted out the notes, told her when he wanted the cakes delivered and then asked if she would mind seeing him to the door.

'I think it must be my eye being covered,' he said, as Mrs Craig escorted him to the garden gate. 'I seem to have lost my sense of balance completely. Good day to you madam.'

Mrs Craig returned to the kitchen and sat down and stared at the money as though she were afraid that it might suddenly vanish. She was still trying to puzzle out what her strange visitor had been talking about when the children returned.

'Mum,' said Johnny at once, 'is Mr Antrobus very rich?'

'I've no idea,' said Mrs Craig, 'in fact I don't even know what he does exactly, and anyway Johnny, it's no business of ours.'

'Where did all that money come from?' asked Lorna, staring at the pound notes.

'From your friend Mr Grant. Which reminds me, he came here enquiring about some bottle which he seemed to think was extremely valuable. What bottle?'

'A bottle I found on the beach,' said Johnny, putting the table cloth straight, 'Mr Grant thought it was smashing and...'

'He was kind about it because we wouldn't let him pay for his tea,' rushed in Alan. 'You see there was this dog...'

'Oh I see,' said Mrs Craig, 'it was one of Johnny's finds was it? You might have let me see it dear, I suppose Mr Grant was trying to find a tactful way of thanking you. Now who's this Mr Chinn?'

'He's a visitor from under the sea,' said Johnny.

'Overseas dear. Another holiday maker, really you have been having a busy time what with all these callers and the mad dog.'

'Forgot about that,' mumbled Alan who had just caught sight of the Djinn's clothes in a pile on the floor.

'Yes, you may well stare,' agreed Mrs Craig picking up the trousers and shaking them, 'I found these under your bed Johnny.'

'Sorry. I'll put them away for you,' said Johnny.

And to everybody's astonishment he took the clothes and hung them neatly over the back of a chair. Then he picked up some of the shopping which had rolled out of the basket and stacked the packets and tins in neat rows on the larder shelves.

'What's the matter with you?' asked Lorna, finding her tongue.

'I like things neat,' said Johnny and went to look for the Djinn.

'Well!' exclaimed Mrs Craig, 'what a day of surprises this is being. Only half an hour ago I was wishing that Johnny would learn to be tidier and now it almost looks as if my wish had been granted.'

'Yes, doesn't it,' Alan said huskily, 'Mum it looks like rain, the washing'll get wet.'

'But it's a lovely day, dear.'

'Clouds coming,' said Alan and fairly pushed his mother out into the garden and shut the door behind her. 'Djinn, Djinn,' he said urgently, 'where are you? Please come out.'

'I'm in here. Atishoo,' said a muffled voice from the vacuum cleaner. 'Inside this terrible monster.'

'Well come out,' said Alan in an agony of impatience.

'Can't. Got no clothes.'

Alan looked desperately at Lorna who was gaping at the cleaner. She pulled herself together and ran upstairs, reappearing a few seconds later with a bundle of very creased green clothes.

'They're not ironed,' she said breathlessly.

'Can't be helped,' Alan replied.

He pushed the cleaner into the corner cupboard and bundled the clothes in after them. He unzipped the dust bag, letting out a great deal of dirt as he did so.

'Hurry, please hurry,' he pleaded.

He shut the door and leant against it and then nodded to Lorna.

'Keep Mum talking out there,' he ordered.

'What about?' asked Lorna, moving from foot to foot.

'Anything, it doesn't matter. Just go *on*.'

'The Djinn's left,' said Johnny appearing on the stairs, 'I wish I knew where he'd gone.' There was a thump from inside the cupboard and Johnny's frown vanished and he added happily, 'Oh of course he's in there.'

'Don't,' said Alan, clapping his hand over his brother's mouth, 'don't wish *anything*. Oh I never thought of that. I wonder what else she wished for.'

'Leggo,' said Johnny wriggling. 'Who?'

'Mum,' said Alan wretchedly. 'Don't you see, all the time we've been OUT, she's been IN—with him. She could've wished for anything. *Now* do you see?'

'Oh goodness,' said Johnny, 'so she could!'

6. *Mr Antrobus*

'I CAN'T,' the Djinn said in his soft sing-song voice, 'we're not *allowed* to tell what other people wished, so it's no good you asking me about your esteemed mother.'

'What's esteemed?' asked Johnny.

'Honoured,' Alan replied, 'it's a very polite way of saying things. But Djinn *why* aren't you allowed to tell?'

The Djinn stopped washing his very dusty face and sat down cross-legged on the bathroom stool.

'Because it leads to many difficulties,' he said. 'Once upon a time, two Mighty Djinns were the slaves of two warring Sheiks. One sheik commanded a great sandstorm to destroy his enemy. When his enemy heard from the Djinns—one told the other while they were having a little gossip one evening—what had caused the storm, *he* wished it back on the first sheik. And *he* returned the storm yet again. For one hundred days and nights that storm rolled backwards and forwards across the desert until all the neighbouring tribes became so angry they threatened to band together to fight both sheiks. And frankly I don't blame them, there was sand everywhere, even in the sherbert.'

'What happened then?' asked Lorna who was cleaning her teeth at the basin.

'A truce was declared and the Djinns had a conference and it was decided that we should never discuss our masters' wishes. So you see...'

'Well at least one of Mum's wishes has come true,' Lorna said later when she was trying to cheer up Alan, 'Johnny's turned tidy. So perhaps the Wicked Land-Lord'll write tomorrow.'

But the Wicked Landlord remained obstinately silent and the postman never came within sight of the Water Tower. Mrs Craig bought a great many things from the Sandstone Dairy and she and Lorna spent two days mixing and baking and icing and the house was full of wonderful smells.

'It reminds me of the Old Days,' said the Djinn,

sniffing at the top of the stairs, 'ah, what feasts we used to have. Mounds of rice all sticky with dates and honey. Lambs turning on spits, sheeps' eyes...'

'Eeeuuurr,' said Johnny.

'A great delicacy,' the Djinn said, quite severely for him, 'your food doesn't smell like ours used to.'

When everything was finished and packed in boxes, Mrs Craig looked quite pretty and flushed and more like her old self.

'Although I shouldn't say it,' she remarked, 'I think Mr Grant ought to be pleased. Now then children, you're to deliver these to him personally at the hotel and don't forget to thank him for the pound each that he's given you.'

'He didn't, you did,' said Alan, 'out of the cake money. Couldn't it go towards the rent?'

'I've put some aside for that dear. Now here are your Post Office Savings Books, you're to put the money straight into them.'

'All of it?' asked Lorna.

'You can keep out half-a-crown each then. You must save the rest for a rainy day because remember money doesn't grow on trees.'

Johnny grinned and Lorna giggled, but Mrs Craig was packing the boxes into a basket and didn't notice.

There was so much to carry that neither Alan nor Lorna saw that Johnny had a suspiciously large bulge in the pocket of his raincoat. His hair was neatly brushed and he was wearing his shoes on the correct feet.

'You don't look a bit like you,' said Lorna, who rather missed the old untidy Johnny, although this one was much easier to look after.

'Who do I look like then?' said Johnny reasonably

enough. Lorna sniffed and Alan went up to have a last word with the Djinn who was to spend the afternoon in the tank room at the very top of the tower.

'I'm going to the Post Office to ask Miss Pockett about sending you as a registered parcel,' he said. 'I should think seven and sixpence might just about cover it.'

'Very kind,' said the Djinn, who was trying to get the curl back into the limp toes of his long shoes. 'The only trouble is...'

'Yes,' said Alan, pausing impatiently in the doorway.

'Nothing,' said the Djinn with a mournful smile, 'may the Djinns of the Marsh Land travel with you.'

He watched them as they set out down the bumpy road and shook his head. What he hadn't liked to mention was that Alan would have to send the parcel *to* somebody and that somebody would have to open it to let the Djinn out.

'Ah me,' sighed the Djinn and picked up the two hair rollers which Lorna had borrowed for him and began to wind the pointed toes of his shoes round them. 'Ah me.'

The children hadn't been inside the Hotel for a long time, not since their father had died and they had forgotten how large and grand it was. Alan went in first with Lorna practically treading on his heels, her eyes fixed on the shopping basket and Johnny trailed along in the rear having a good look at everything. It made him think of the Water Tower in a way, for it seemed to be very empty with just two old ladies sitting in one corner of the big lounge. An elderly waiter was laying up the tea tables and there was a ginger cat asleep in front of the coal fire. There was nobody behind the reception desk so Alan coughed and then knocked softly on the counter.

'There's a bell,' said Lorna, nudging him.

'You ring it then.'

'No you.'

'I will,' said Johnny and did, very loudly. The cat opened its eyes and stretched and the two old ladies stared. A young lady with very fair hair and a bored face came out of an inner office and said:

'Well?'

'We've got something for Mr Grant.' said Alan in a low voice.

'Speak up, I can't hear you.'

'MR GRANT.'

'There's no need to shout,' she said crossly, 'you can't see him, he's in bed.'

'What's the matter with him?' Lorna asked, forgetting to be shy.

'He sprained his ankle. You can leave those things here, he told me you'd be calling.'

'I want to see him,' said Lorna with surprising firmness. In fact she wanted Mr Grant to see the cake which she had iced with such care.

'Oh very well,' the fair-haired lady said, even more crossly, 'he's in Room One at the top of the stairs.' She turned and went back into her office and the children heard her say, 'Nobody important, only some scruffy kids.'

Lorna went pink and then white, because she had put on her best Sunday coat specially and even if it was rather short there was no need for people to make nasty remarks.

'When I'm grown up,' she said in a low voice as they climbed the thickly carpeted stairs, 'I'm going to be nice about *everybody*.'

Alan knocked on the door of Number One and after a pause a faint, dreamy voice said, 'Come in.'

The room was in half-darkness because all the curtains were drawn and for a moment no one could see anything and then they noticed a bed with a shadowy mound in it so they all trooped across to it.

'Mind the rug,' said Mr Grant, 'that's what I tripped over.'

'Does your ankle hurt a lot?' asked Lorna, feeling for the edge of a chair and putting down the baskets.

'Not really, thank you.'

There was a silence during which everybody fidgeted and then Mr Grant seemed to rouse himself a little and he put up his hand and turned on the light which made everybody blink. He looked paler and more miserable than ever, but when he saw the children staring at him anxiously he managed to smile.

'So you've brought the cakes, good.'

Lorna unpacked them and arranged them on the bedside table and Mr Grant looked at them and nodded, but he wasn't nearly as pleased as Lorna had hoped he would be after all the trouble she had taken.

'Very nice,' he said faintly, 'I'm sure they'll be a great success.'

'It's chocolate icing and it's got *three* layers,' Lorna said.

'It sounds wonderful,' said Mr Grant and lay back and gazed at the ceiling.

'Yes, well,' said Alan shuffling his feet and wondering how they could say goodbye.

'About that bottle,' Johnny said suddenly, 'do you still want to buy it?'

'Not at the moment,' said Mr Grant shutting his eyes, 'I feel a little tired. Some other time perhaps.'

'Thank you for the pound,' said Lorna stiffly, 'Mum gave us all a share out of the cake money.'

'Not at all, not at all. Thank you for the cakes,' said Mr Grant his voice dying away into a whisper and everybody backed out of the door as quickly as they could.

'Do you think he's going to die?' Lorna whispered.

'People don't die from bad ankles,' said Alan far more firmly than he felt. 'Come on, let's go and see Miss Pockett.'

'I'm going somewhere else,' said Johnny as soon as they were out in the street which was pleasantly noisy and full of people after the quiet emptiness of the Hotel.

'Where?'

'To see a friend.'

'What friend?'

'My friend.'

'Yes, but *what* friend?'

'Oh never mind him,' said Alan who knew it was no good asking Johnny questions if he didn't feel like answering them. 'Only don't be long that's all.'

Johnny nodded and went off down the street with his hand firmly holding something inside his pocket. He and the Djinn had had a long and interesting talk and Johnny had slowly, but firmly made his mind up about what had to be done. It was no good talking it over with Alan and Lorna because they hardly ever agreed with what he wanted to do, so he was going ahead on his own. He thought of his lovely money tree and shook his head. Some people just didn't know a good idea when they saw it.

Mr Antrobus's strange house was dozing in the faint afternoon sunshine and Johnny, instead of knocking on the front door, went down an alley and let himself into the yard at the back. He and Mr Antrobus were old friends and Johnny approved of him because, like the Djinn, he didn't ask a lot of silly questions.

Mr Antrobus was in the kitchen searching for something and when Johnny appeared on the step, Mr Antrobus said:

'Dratted kettle.'

Johnny nodded and began to search among the pots and pans until he found the kettle inside the oven. He handed it silently to Mr Antrobus who nodded in his turn and filled it at the sink.

'Are you very rich?' asked Johnny.

Mr Antrobus wrinkled up his round, fat face until his eyes almost vanished and then scratched his bald head.

'Depends what you mean by rich,' he said, 'I'm rich compared to a herring, poor compared to my Bank Manager. Does that answer your question?'

Johnny sucked in his mouth and thought deeply, then he brought his hand out of his coat pocket and put the Djinn's bottle down on the kitchen table.

'Will you pay me a lot of money for that?' he asked.

'God bless my soul,' said Mr Antrobus, reaching for his spectacles which were perched high on his forehead. 'And where did you get this, if you don't mind my asking?'

'Found it. Beach.'

'Really?'

Mr Antrobus pushed his spectacles up again and held the bottle close to his eyes.

'Eekynocks. Low tide,' said Johnny, feeling that more explanation was called for.

'Equinox,' said Mr Antrobus musingly, 'what a piece of luck. What a stroke of good fortune. Well I'll be honest with you Johnny. If I were a rich man I would pay you quite a lot of money for this. But I'm not so I can't. See?'

Johnny stared at him for some time in unblinking silence and Mr Antrobus sat down on the creaking settle and stared back.

'It's the Wicked Landlord is it?' he asked at last.

'Yes.'

'I'm sorry,' Mr Antrobus said, 'sincerely sorry. If I could help you I would, but this bottle must be worth at least fifty pounds, perhaps more. If I paid you anything less I'd be cheating you. Do you understand?'

'Yes,' said Johnny heavily, 'I'd better go now.'

'Hold on a moment,' said Mr Antrobus, 'I suppose I could pay you by instalments after all my luck may turn.'

'It doesn't matter,' said Johnny, who didn't understand what Mr Antrobus meant. He picked up the bottle and made for the door.

'I thought you was rich because you work such a lot,' he said from the step.

'A great many people work hard without ever making a great deal of money,' said Mr Antrobus. 'It all depends what you do. Wicked Landlords for instance own a great many houses and all those houses pay rent. But all I do is write.'

'Stories?' said Johnny, who thought it was a funny way to make a living. He hated writing anything himself.

Mr Antrobus pursed his mouth into a small round 'O' and looked over his shoulder. Then he beckoned to Johnny to come closer and whispered in his ear.

'Those little books on local beauty spots. I think I've got one here somewhere,' and he scrabbled among the tins of beans and packets of spaghetti and produced a very thin paper covered book called *Sandstone—Pearl of the South Coast*. It had a very brightly coloured picture of the High Street on the front and all the houses looked as if they were about to fall over.

'Awful isn't it?' said Mr Antrobus with pride. 'Listen to how it starts. "Friends, if your footsteps—or should I say your car wheels—should take you across the great marsh of Kent, be sure and call in at Sandstone. For Sandstone is a veritable storehouse of treasure and interest to all seekers after beauty." There!'

'What does it mean exactly?' asked Johnny after a very long pause.

'Nothing,' said Mr Antrobus quite gaily, 'it's a lot of nonsense, but people buy it all the same. Just like they buy hideous little ashtrays with a Present from Sandstone written on the bottom. Or stickers for their car windows which say "We've been sunning ourselves at Sandstone." Old Pockett sells those by the hundred. But don't ask me *who* buys them or *why*, it's all a mystery to me. Still it pays the butcher's bill. All the same Johnny, I'd rather you didn't tell anyone else that I write these things. I don't sign them you see, they just have my initials, H. A. on the cover.'

'All right,' said Johnny, 'what's H for?'

'Horatio. I'd rather keep that dark too. Are you sure you won't stay for tea?'

'No thank you. Well goodbye.'

'You could take that bottle to an antique dealer.'

'P'raps.'

'Hang on to it,' said Mr Antrobus in a muffled voice as he was now half inside the kitchen cabinet looking for the milk, 'for a bit and we'll see what I can do. But treat it gently.'

Johnny nodded and marched off to join the others.

He had quite a lot to think over and although he had been disappointed at the failure of his plan—neither Mr Grant nor Mr Antrobus had done what he wanted —Johnny was not finished yet.

Alan and Lorna had met with a disappointment too, for Miss Pockett at the Post Office had told them quite firmly that any parcel going registered Airmail to Arabia was going to cost more than seven shillings and sixpence.

'Isn't it funny how everything always seems to come back to money,' said Alan as they walked back across the marsh.

'Oh I wish we had thousands and thousands of pounds,' said Lorna.

'Don't,' said Alan. 'At least not while the Djinn's around. There'd be something wrong with it for certain. And that goes for you too, Johnny. Don't you dare wish unless we've talked about it first.'

'No,' said Johnny, crossing his fingers inside his pocket, 'no, all right. Race you home.'

And he set off down the road with the Djinn's bottle bumping backwards and forwards against his leg.

7. *A Treat for the Djinn*

'THERE,' said Lorna, 'that doesn't look half bad. See for yourself.'

The Djinn was sitting in the tank room with a towel

draped round his shoulders. He was wearing a sweater belonging to Alan, a pair of rather baggy trousers which had once been Mr Craig's and Johnny's second best shoes. His face was no longer pale green, but a somewhat unusual shade of pink, for Lorna had just finished coating it with some of her mother's powder.

For some days the Djinn had been growing steadily more and more sad. He had tried to disguise the fact, but Lorna had noticed it and had dragged the truth out of him.

'I'm a failure,' the Djinn sighed, staring out across the rippling grass on the marsh. 'There has been no word from your Wicked Landlord, when I made the money tree it was the wrong sort of money, Johnny is very tidy but everybody dislikes it and people are afraid of me.'

'We're not,' Lorna said truthfully, 'we like you very much.'

'You're different,' said the Djinn, 'you understand. But you have to hide me from your mother and Mr Grant seemed very upset when *he* saw me. Oh dear, oh dear.'

'I think he's getting very bored being shut up in the tank room all the time,' Lorna confided to Alan.

'I've given him all my old comics,' Johnny said.

'Yes, but he can't read them, he only looks at the pictures. Think how cross you get if you have to stay in bed when you're ill, and he's perfectly well.'

'We can't take him out with us,' said Alan, 'because of his green face and because of people wishing for things.'

It was then that Lorna had her great idea.

'Then we'll change how he looks,' she said. 'Leave it to me.'

Now, considering the results of her efforts, she wasn't quite so sure. The Djinn still looked rather unusual, but at least he was no longer pale green, but bright pink.

'Will it come off?' he asked anxiously.

'Only if you wash it,' Lorna reassured him, 'now we're all going to a party and you'll have a lovely time and forget all about being a failure. That is,' she corrected herself quickly, 'thinking that you're a failure.'

'Some party,' Alan whispered to Johnny, 'the Bring and Buy Sale in the church hall, still I suppose it's better than nothing.'

The Djinn got up and began walking round the room with small shuffling steps for although the shoes were not as heavy or ungainly as the gumboots they still felt rather cumbersome and strange after his light Arabian shoes.

'There's just one thing,' Alan said, looking slightly uncomfortable, 'would you mind wearing these in your ears?' And he produced two fluffy pieces of cotton wool. 'You see it'll stop you hearing people if they suddenly start wishing for things.'

'Certainly,' the Djinn replied with quiet dignity, 'I understand perfectly,' and he put the cotton wool in his pointed ears underneath the knitted hat which had taken the place of his turban for the afternoon.

Mrs Craig and Lorna were going on ahead to the church hall where the tea was being held to help with putting out the food. Lorna had made several of her boxes decorated with sea-shells and as the Djinn had helped her to paint them in delicate shades of pale blue and green they looked very attractive.

But, as Alan said in an aside to Johnny, 'They're all right now, but wait till they get that funny seaweedy smell.'

'Oh I wish they wouldn't, I can't understand why they do,' said Lorna, overhearing this remark and as all of them had forgotten that the Djinn was in the room at the time—he was the sort of person that it's very easy to overlook once you get used to having them about the place—he had blown himself up very quietly, muttered and shivered, so of course the boxes never would smell which was very lucky for the kind people who finally bought them.

Alan gave his mother and Lorna half an hour's start and then set off with Johnny and the Djinn. The Djinn was quite nervous with excitement at this journey into the outside world and as his own deafness made him shout, the boys had a difficult time trying to make him calm down.

'The fish,' the Djinn said loudly, slithering along between the boys, 'told me of many wonders in your new world. Of the great silver fish that fly through the air with mighty noises.'

'Aeroplanes,' shouted Alan.

'And the great fish which travel over the land and also make a great deal of noise.'

'Cars,' roared Johnny.

'And of a fearsome fish which roars over the water. They all hated that and many of them moved away. It came close to me once,' the Djinn said, skipping to keep up and shouting at the top of his sing-song voice, 'and it was indeed a dreadful thing.'

'You mean on the water,' Alan shouted.

'What?' said the Djinn, cupping his hand to his hidden ear.

'ON THE WATER,' Alan bellowed back so loudly that a nearby sheep who had been watching them placidly, kicked up its feet and went trotting off to another part of the marsh.

'Over the water,' the Djinn shouted back, 'a great round fish,' and he threw his arms about trying to give an imitation.

'He means the hovercraft at Ramsgate,' said Alan, 'and he's quite right too, it does make the most awful row. You can hear it right over on the North Foreland. No wonder the fishing's got so bad if it's scared them all away. Now then Djinn,' and he tapped him on the shoulder.

The Djinn, who had been staring across the marsh, jumped violently and looked round.

'What is THAT!' he demanded.

Alan looked in the direction of his pointing finger and then mouthing the words very carefully he tried to explain about the small track Dungeness railway. The Djinn watched him carefully, but although he nodded and smiled in his usual polite manner they could tell by the crease between his green eyes, that he was none the wiser at the end of it.

'Perhaps we shouldn't be taking him after all,' said Alan doubtfully.

'Too late,' said Johnny, 'we're there.'

It was early closing day in Sandstone so the shops had their shutters down which gave the High Street a sleepy look, but there were quite a number of people about, all of them making in the direction of the Church Hall. It was a rather ugly building with a tin roof which made a hammering noise if it rained hard. There was a large placard over the door which read:

Bring and Buy

OLD FOLKS TEA FREE OF CHARGE

PRIZES . BARGAINS. ADMISSION 6d

Miss Pockett from the Post Office was standing in the doorway behind a rather rickety green-topped table on which were arranged a reel of tickets and a saucer full of money. Miss Pockett herself was small and bright and was wearing a large hat with a great deal of pink veiling about it.

'Hallo,' she said, 'how NICE to see you. I don't see how I can charge you when your mother and Lorna are helping and...' her voice trailed away as she caught sight of the Djinn who was staring at her with equal interest.

'He's a foreigner,' said Alan, who had thought all this out well in advance.

'Oh a TOURIST,' said Miss Pocket, 'it's a little EARLY in the season for them isn't it? That'll be sixpence sir.'

The Djinn put his hands together and bowed and Alan hastily slid some money into the saucer and took the Djinn's arm and drew him into the hall. Although it was not a very warm day the inside of the hall was already rather hot and full of noise as everybody was talking at once.

'It is like the souk,' said the Djinn, his eyes lighting up.

'The what?' asked Alan, who had caught sight of his mother behind the tea-urn.

'Souk,' shouted the Djinn, his teeth flashing in a wide smile, 'Arabian market. It is very nice, oh it reminds me of home. Everybody bargaining so!'

'Yes, I daresay,' said Alan, who was already starting

to feel harassed. 'Come on, over here,' and he led the way towards the Fancy Goods stall which Miss Pockett's father was looking after. He was very old and when the tourists came to Sandstone in the summer he usually sat on the bench outside the Smugglers Rest with his chin resting on a knobbly stick. He had special summer clothes which consisted of a moleskin jacket, breeches, highly polished gaiters and a hat with the brim turned down all the way round. When the tourists saw him with his neat white beard and wrinkled patient face they usually hurried across to take his photograph. Old Mr Pockett was very shy about having his picture taken and it sometimes cost the tourists a shilling before he'd let them do it. Even then he sometimes got muddled about the difference between a two shilling piece and a half-crown.

During the winter months, however, he was quite different. He wore clothes which were just like anybody else's and helped his daughter in the Post Office. He was sharp enough then about two shilling pieces which often puzzled Alan.

'Roll up, roll up,' he said when he saw Alan and Johnny. 'Well then and how are you? Going to send any more parcels to Araby?' and he laughed so hard that he caught his breath and choked.

'We haven't sent any yet,' said Alan, who was afraid his mother might hear.

'What can I interest you in?' asked Mr Pockett, who never bothered to listen to what people said to him unless they wanted to take his photograph. 'Buy your Mum a present why don't you? There's a lovely shell box here, just the thing, do her proud so it would. Real craftsmanship that is.'

'Lorna made it,' said Johnny.

'Or how about a nice letter rack? Or a kettle holder? Leastways I think it's a holder.'

The Djinn, who had been gazing with great admiration at Mr Pockett, put out his hand and the next moment he found the kettle holder pressed into it and a cash box being rattled under his nose.

'Two and frepence,' said Mr Pockett, 'and a bargain at the price.'

'No, no sir,' the Djinn shouted, 'not that one if you please kind sir. That one.'

'Furriner?' said Mr Pockett, his voice dropping to a quaver, 'I can't hear you sir. What is it you want?'

'That,' said the Djinn pointing, his eyes glowing like emeralds.

'What's that then?' asked Mr Pockett, 'the candle stick? No? Bless me if I ever see such a chap. You show me, sir, what it is you're after.'

The Djinn, who found it difficult with the cotton-wool in his ears, to follow what Mr Pockett was saying, looked to Alan for help.

'Deaf,' Alan shouted to Mr Pockett and then to the Djinn, 'What is it?'

The Djinn leant over the stall and picked up a large clumsy ring which was nestling among a group of purple egg cosies. He waved it at Mr Pockett who said:

'Bless us all, it's a funny sort of a thing to pick. Given by a friend of mine that was, a very learned gentleman. Yes, very nice sir. A very handsome piece and worth a fair lot too. Antikuee.'

'It's got ninepence on the label,' said Johnny.

Mr Pockett gave him a sharper look and then smiled at the Djinn who was staring at the ring which he was cradling in his hands. He was trembling violently and

Alan wondered if all the excitement was proving too much for him. His face was already getting a strange streaky look in the heat. Alan said quickly, 'Ninepence, I'll pay.'

He gave Mr Pockett a shilling and the old man put it slowly into the cashbox and even more slowly counted out six halfpennies in change.

'What do you want that silly old ring for?' asked Alan, dragging the Djinn away from Mr Pockett who had started staring at the Djinn's pale green hands.

'Why shouldn't he buy that ring if he wants it?' said Johnny.

'Yoo, hoo, Alan,' Mrs Craig called from behind the urn, 'come and give us a hand dear.'

'Oh bother,' Alan said distractedly. He took hold of Johnny's arm and added in a fierce whisper, 'You'll have to look after him. Don't let him out of your sight. Promise!'

Johnny nodded and Alan slid through the crowds towards his mother leaving Johnny to push and elbow the Djinn to one side of the hall where it was a bit quieter.

'Never you mind,' said Johnny, 'I think it's a very nice ring.'

'It is his,' whispered the Djinn, turning it over and over.

'Whose?'

'My master's,' said the Djinn, lip reading. 'This is the ring of my dead master. The one who brought me to this land from Arabia. See it has his markings on the side.'

And he turned the ring over and with trembling pale green fingers he traced the two small letters engraved in the metal.

'H A' Johnny read out, 'that's funny, I've seen that somewhere else.'

'Hallo,' said a familiar wheezy voice from behind them, 'I thought I'd find you hereabouts. I want a word with you, Johnny, my lad.'

And Mr Antrobus laid one fat finger against the side of his nose and winked solemnly.

8. A Little Bit of Luck

THE Vicar climbed up on to the platform at the end of the hall and made a short speech in which he welcomed everybody to the Sale, asked them to spend as much money as they could as it was for a good cause and then said tea was now being served. There was a sudden surge forwards and Alan, who had been looking round anxiously for the Djinn and Johnny was swept backwards until he came to rest against Mr Pockett's stall.

'Adiy-oop,' said Mr Pockett, 'allus the same when it's tea-time. You'd think some of 'em hadn't had a bite for a week. Where's your foreign friend then?'

'With Johnny,' said Alan, standing on tip-toe and trying to look over the heads of the crowd.

'Funny sort of chap, no offence meant and none taken I hope,' said Mr Pockett, 'I suppose it's being foreign as does it. I hear you're in a proper pickle up at the Tower.'

'What!'

'No need to jump down my throat boy. You can't keep nothing to yourself in a place this size.'

'You mean, you *know?*' asked Alan, swallowing.

'Things get about. Shame it is, putting up the rent and making it so difficult for a nice woman like your mother.'

'Oh *that*. Yes it is,' Alan agreed with a sigh of relief.

'I heard a rumour,' said Mr Pockett and then stopped, 'well never mind that now. Seeing as how you're here and I'm feeling a bit peckish would you look after the stall for me? Everything's marked and that.'

'I want to find Johnny...' Alan began.

'Good, good,' said Mr Pockett, 'I knew you'd do it. Mind you count the change proper. Shan't be long.'

And he wriggled off through the crowds as easily as a snake travelling through grass. Alan put the cashbox down on the ground for safety and watched the people edging past. He felt a little shy at first, but nobody seemed to take much notice of him except the Vicar who said in a loud voice how splendid it was to see the Young helping with a Good Cause. At which Alan went scarlet and pretended to be very busy putting the things on the stall tidy. He sold a pair of Lorna's boxes to the two old ladies from the Hotel and all the purple egg cosies to a very small girl who paid for them in pennies.

'It's for me Mum,' she said, counting out the money very slowly, 'it's her birthday and she loves pretty things.'

'What an extraordinary collection of junk,' said a bored voice. The little girl and Alan looked up and there was the fair-haired lady from the Hotel wearing a very smart hat and coat and her usual cross expression. In a strange sort of way her words made all the goods on the stall seem dull and shabby and even the purple cosies lost some of their bright colour. The little girl looked at them with an expression of doubt, her smile vanishing.

'I think they're jolly nice too,' said Alan loudly, 'look, there's a teapot cover to match,' and he brought it out from the back of the stall. There was a china lady on the top of it and her woollen skirt was the tea cosy.

'Oh it is lovely,' the little girl agreed, her eyes lighting up again, 'but I expect it's ever so expensive and I've only got sixpence left.'

'That's exactly what it costs,' said Alan, telling a white lie. And he undid the label which had two and sixpence written on it and handed the cosy to the little girl. 'It's a real bargain,' he added, which was perfectly true.

'I'll have it then,' said the little girl.

The lady from the hotel raised her eyebrows and moved on and Alan did up the egg cosies and the teapot cover in a parcel with a great deal of sticky tape. The little girl went off hugging her present and Alan felt in his own pocket for two shillings to make up the difference in the price.

'Good afternoon,' said Mr Grant, suddenly looming up in front of the stall. 'How's trade?'

'Quite good thank you.'

Mr Grant, who was walking with a stick and who still looked pale and ill, stayed to buy a book called *Ramble Across Romney Marsh With Me* by 'H. A.' and then went off leaving it behind.

'Hi,' Alan called, waving the book above his head.

'All right, all right,' said Mr Pockett slipping through the crowd, 'I'm coming. Very good tea that was, but not enough of it. How's tricks?'

'Can I go now?' Alan asked.

'I seen young Johnny,' said Mr Pockett, who was mopping his face with a yellow handkerchief. 'He's out round the back with that foreign chap.'

The air outside was pleasantly cool and clear after the heat in the hall and Alan stopped for a moment to get his breath back. Lorna came running up behind him looking very hot and with chocolate all round her mouth.

'You might have come and helped us,' she said reproachfully, 'it was awful with everybody pushing and shoving. Much worse than the holiday people in the summer.'

'I was looking after Mr Pockett's stall,' said Alan. 'Have you seen the Djinn?'

'Mr Pockett ate *ten* cakes. No, I haven't seen the Djinn, but Mum has. She was asking Mr Grant about him.'

'?' said Alan.

'It's all right,' said Lorna cheerfully, 'he was in one of his funny moods. He didn't seem to understand what she was talking about half the time. And then he nearly upset the urn and he got hot tea all down himself and Mum had to take him over to the Vicarage to sponge him down. He said he wasn't burnt, but he looked awful. All wobbly.'

Alan was only half listening because he'd just caught sight of Johnny and the Djinn and Mr Antrobus walking backwards and forwards across the piece of wasteland round the corner from the hall. They were all talking and nodding and Alan realised at once that the Djinn must have taken out his earplugs and his heart sank.

'Quite astonishing,' Mr Antrobus was saying as Alan and Lorna caught up with him, 'after seeing that bottle of yours it occurred to me that some time ago I had noticed something of a similar nature in my own house. Usually I can put my hand on anything. I'm very methodical by nature.'

'Methodical?' said Johnny.

'Tidy,' said Mr Antrobus, 'In my mind. It's a great gift. What was I saying?'

'You were referring to the bottle, sir,' the Djinn prompted him.

'Ah yes, so I began to have a little search among my goods and chattels. Belongings,' he added hastily as Johnny's mouth opened, 'and at length, at last, I found not a bottle, dear me no, but an old notebook. It was quite fascinating.'

'Interesting,' said Alan as Johnny looked at him.

'It was very old and rather worn. Some of the pages were quite crumbly at the edges,' Mr Antrobus went on, 'and the ink was very faded, but I stayed up all night reading it. Guess what it was?'

Four faces looked at him blankly and Mr Antrobus gave a contented wheezy laugh.

'It was the journal of a sorcerer.'

'Oh no,' said the Djinn, his voice rising, 'surely not? An alchemist perhaps, or a magician.'

'Have it your own way,' said Mr Antrobus good-naturedly, 'I was so interested that I sat down there and then and wrote an article about it. It was, though I say it myself, a fine piece of writing. I sent it off to a magazine called *Country Chat* and,' he paused panting a little for he was very fat and not used to exercise, 'and they bought it and paid me handsomely into the bargain. What do you think of that for a bit of luck?'

'Smashing,' said Alan.

'Lovely,' agreed Lorna.

'A lot of money?' asked Johnny before anyone could stop him.

'A fair amount,' Mr Antrobus replied, 'but, what is even better, they have asked me to write some more. A whole series of articles. It's like a dream come true.'

'I'm so glad,' Lorna said warmly.

'Me too,' Alan agreed and then he noticed that both Johnny and the Djinn were looking rather strange and a sudden idea came into his mind.

'I am delighted sir, at your good fortune,' said the Djinn, avoiding Alan's eyes.

'Thank you, thank you,' Mr Antrobus said, 'Do you know it's most odd but I have the feeling that we have met before. Is that possible?'

'No, no,' the Djinn said, 'I have only recently returned from, from somewhere else.'

'Strange,' said Mr Antrobus, 'I wish I could think where it...'

'Tea,' said Alan very loudly, 'have you had any tea Mr Antrobus?'

'There are some very nice cakes,' Lorna said, backing

him up while the Djinn quivered on the edge of Mr Antrobus's wish, 'Mummy and I made them.'

'Well in that case, I shall have to sample a few before they're all gone,' Mr Antrobus said.

Lorna firmly took hold of his arm and dragged him towards the hall and Alan fell behind to have a word with the Djinn.

'You promised not to take out the cotton wool,' he said in a low voice.

'I'm so sorry,' the Djinn hung his head, 'but it was the excitement of finding my master's ring. I hoped that I should learn from it whence it came, but I was unable to find the aged one who sold it to me. To you, that is. It is really yours,' and he took it out of his pocket and offered it to Alan.

'No you keep it, boys don't wear rings these days. Johnny did you make a wish about Mr Antrobus?'

'Sort of,' said Johnny. The Djinn looked up at the evening sky and began to whistle.

'I thought I told you...'

'We worked it out together,' Johnny said quickly, 'me and the Djinn so that I got all the words right. I just wished for him to be famous and rich in an ordinary way and now he is. How much is tea?'

'I suppose it's all right then,' Alan said doubtfully, 'I don't know about tea. I'll see how much I've got. That's odd.'

'What?' asked Johnny, glad to have cleared that difficulty with so little trouble. He winked at the Djinn.

'I've got two shillings in my pocket,' said Alan slowly, 'I paid sixpence for the Djinn to get in and ninepence for the ring, that's one and threepence and two shillings for—for something else.'

'What?'

'Just something,' said Alan, thinking of the purple teacosy, 'so that's three and threepence and I only had that much to start with, but I've got two shillings left.'

'Let's have some tea then,' said Johnny who wasn't really interested, 'I'm starving.'

They joined Lorna and Mr Antrobus at one of the small card tables and Alan, who was still puzzling over his unexpected find, forgot to ask the Djinn to put back his cotton wool ear plugs.

'My treat,' said Mr Antrobus, 'I'm in a spending mood today,' and he smiled at Johnny who looked very pleased with himself. Mr Antrobus handed over a pound note and Lorna and Johnny went off to load up a couple of trays with food and cups of very pale tea.

'Tell me sir,' Mr Antrobus said to the Djinn, 'are you staying long in this country?'

'I don't know,' said the Djinn, glancing nervously at Alan.

'I've always wanted to travel myself,' said Mr Antrobus thoughtfully. 'Too old for it now, of course. Pity. May I ask where you come from?'

'Arabia, sir,' the Djinn said, 'it is such a beautiful country. Ah shall I ever see again the trackless deserts, the cool oases, the long jingling camel trains, the graceful palm trees?'

'Well I'm sure I hope you will,' said Mr Antrobus. 'It sounds fascinating. Funny, I never thought of Arabia as quite like that.'

'Tea,' said Lorna, 'do have one of these cakes. I made them.'

'Delicious,' said Mr Antrobus, eating one in two bites. 'Quite melts in the mouth. You know I wish that I...'

And then luckily Miss Pockett came up to the table to clear away some of the dirty plates.

'It's all been SUCH a success,' she said, 'Thank you Johnny dear, that is KIND.' For the new, neat Johnny was carefully stacking the crockery in a tidy pile. 'Such good children all of you and a great help to your dear mother. I've heard about your little trouble with the rent and I call it downright WICKED.'

'How *do* people find out?' asked Alan as Miss Pockett marched off.

'Can't keep a secret in a place like this,' said Mr Antrobus, starting on his fourth cake, 'it's all round the town if you've got toothache. Have you heard the latest rumour?'

'What's that?' asked Lorna, who was always interested in hearing any kind of story.

'Just one more of those currant things, I think,' said Mr Antrobus. 'No, no I never repeat rumours. You're not eating sir.'

The Djinn shook his head and by the time Mr Antrobus had finished the hall was nearly deserted and there were very few things left on the stalls. What remained was being sold off so cheaply that Lorna got three tiny notebooks for a penny and Alan a balsam-wood aircraft for his mysterious two shillings.

'I'll fly it from the tankroom,' he said as he helped his mother to clear up the tea stall.

'Mind you don't fly with it,' said Mrs Craig, 'oh dear *what* an afternoon. I wonder who made the most money.'

'Mr Pockett,' said the Vicar, who was busy counting up all the takings, 'it's quite astonishing how he does it. Not a thing left and most of it was rather dull to start with. Except for those pretty boxes of course. Hallo, what's this?'

And he peered at a coin which glinted dully in the electric light.

'Somebody's given him some foreign money by the look of it,' said Mr Antrobus, 'fancy old Pockett not noticing,' and he chuckled.

'Ah well,' said the Vicar, giving Mr Antrobus a cold look, 'at least it's money of a kind and not a button. I've had those in the plate at church before now. Well I'd like to take all you good people back to the Vicarage to partake of a little light refreshment. You deserve a rest from your labours.'

'Well it would be a nice break,' said Mrs Craig with a soft sigh.

Lorna looked at her mother's flushed, but tired face and felt all her old familiar worry sweep over her.

'Do go,' she said quickly, 'we'll finish here. Honestly.'

'Dear child,' said the Vicar patting her head, 'what a kind thought. But no, there's no need to fret. I shall lock up the hall for the night and on the morrow my faithful band of helpers will finish everything. Let us all adjourn to the Vicarage.'

'I'd rather not thank you,' said Alan who could see the Djinn hanging around by the door and who didn't want the Vicar to start asking him questions.

'Alan, that's not very polite,' said Mrs Craig.

'We'll go home and start the supper,' said Lorna who was in a very virtuous mood.

'That's settled then,' said Alan, 'see you later, Mum.'

He nodded to the Djinn who slipped quietly out into the darkness where he was shortly joined by the Craigs and Mr Antrobus.

'Did you enjoy it?' asked Lorna.

'Oh yes indeed,' the Djinn replied, his green eyes shining in the dark like those of a cat. 'It made me think of my home and the market place. Such bargaining, such splendid goods and, thanks to your generous goodness, I have the ring of my master which I shall treasure for always.'

' 'Night all,' shouted Mr Antrobus, letting himself into his house and letting out a shaft of light. He waved to them and then the door was shut and they could hear him humming to himself like a large, sleepy bee.

They walked in silence through the town and out on to the marsh road, their eyes slowly getting used to the dark. They all had a lot to think about and as the wind had dropped and the tide was only half in, it was very quiet.

'What's that?' Lorna said suddenly.

'A cow,' said Alan, listening to the distant moaning sound which seemed to be coming from the beach.

'There aren't any cows round here, it's all sheep,' Lorna replied in a whisper. She and the Djinn moved closer together and the boys, after a moment's hesitation went off to investigate. They could see quite well now for it was a cloudless, starlit night and there was a faint blue glow over everything. The beach looked quite different from usual, much larger and rather wild and desolate with its little humps of rock and the indigo shadows which were clumps of seaweed.

'It's that rock there,' Alan said pointing, 'that's where the noise is.'

'S'not a rock,' said Johnny, 'it's Mr Grant.'

'What's the matter now?' asked Alan, letting out a sigh of relief at the noise being made by something so ordinary. He had become so used to Mr Grant always being in some kind of trouble that he forgot to speak to him as a grown-up.

'My knee,' said Mr Grant in a faint voice, 'I came out for a walk along the sands. It was so calm and peaceful and I was strolling along when suddenly the ground gave way under me.'

'Quicksands,' said Johnny nodding, 'there are lots of little patches round here. They're good for crabs.'

'I tried to save myself,' Mr Grant went on, 'but I fell just the same and I came down most awkwardly on one knee and I must have twisted it. I called and shouted, but nobody answered.'

'Well we have now,' Alan said, 'see if you can get up if we help you. You can use us like crutches.'

'I'll try,' Mr Grant said, not sounding too sure, 'my stick's over there. If you could pass it to me that might help.'

'What is it?' asked Lorna, who had decided that she would rather be with her brothers than alone with the Djinn, who had been shivering and shaking even more than she had.

'Mr Grant,' said Alan, heaving and pulling while Johnny pushed from behind.

'You haven't hurt yourself again!' Lorna said, clicking her tongue against her teeth and sounding exactly like her mother. 'Really I don't know how you manage to be so silly.'

'I know, I know,' agreed Mr Grant, whose face looked even greener than the Djinn's. 'Ouch! Steady.'

He perched on one leg, making Johnny think of the way the seagulls stood sometimes when they were gazing out to sea with their black, unwinking eyes.

'Isn't it lovely out here at night-time?' said Lorna, who had quite forgotten that she had ever been frightened by the empty loneliness of the sands by starlight. And what with one thing and another and because she had had a very busy, important afternoon with people telling her what a good child she was, she suddenly turned a cartwheel, looking like a skinny little starfish with her feet flying through the air.

'Come on and help us,' Alan said impatiently.

'Ah, youth,' said Mr Grant, as though he were a very old man instead of a middle-aged one, 'how I wish that *I* were your age again.'

'No, no, no,' Alan shouted.

But it was too late, the Djinn with a fleeting apologetic glance in his direction had already caught his breath and was muttering furiously.

9. Mr Grant-that-was

ALAN and Johnny fell back and Lorna crouched where she had landed on the sands as Mr Grant shivered and shook in the starlight and then very slowly started to shrink. His arms and legs grew smaller and his head and feet seemed to grow towards each other, quite slowly at first and then faster and faster until he was a little shorter than Alan and a couple of inches taller than Johnny.

'I don't like it,' said Lorna in a whisper and she began to count up to a hundred in quick, breathy gasps.

'I couldn't help it, I couldn't help it,' said the Djinn, bowing up and down very quickly with his hands together.

'He's shrunk,' said Johnny, peering at the figure who was still standing on one leg.

'Will he know what's happened to him?' asked Alan, gripping the Djinn by his shoulders and shaking him backwards and forwards.

'I cannot tell,' gasped the Djinn, his eyes rolling, 'I have never granted this wish before, although there was once a Persian sultan who...'

'Well now,' said the voice of the someone who had once been Mr Grant, 'and who are you?' There had always been a faint lilt in his voice, but now it was much stronger and for a moment nobody undersood what he was saying.

'Who—what?' said Alan, 'Mr Grant I'm awfully sorry, but you see you did wish, didn't you?'

'How do you know my name?' asked Mr Grant-That-Was, 'and anyway who's talking about wishes. I asked a civil question, will you not give me a civil answer?'

'I'm Alan,' said Alan miserably, 'and this is Johnny and that's Lorna over there on the sand. But you know us already, really you do.'

'I do not. I've never seen the lot of you before. Who's yon fellow over there?'

'The Djinn,' said Alan, giving up the struggle and waiting for the worst to happen.

'And what's that when it's at home?'

'My friend,' said Johnny doubling up his fists.

'There's a game one,' said Mr Grant-That-Was, bunching up his own fists. 'Is it a fight you'll be wanting then?'

'All right,' said Johnny and danced towards him. Backwards and forwards across the sand they went, lunging at each other with all their strength, but hardly ever landing a blow because they kept slipping on the seaweed and having to dodge the rocks.

'Johnny stop, oh don't hit him,' said Lorna, trying to grab hold of them, 'Alan stop them.'

But Alan had taken the Djinn to one side and was having a furious whispered conversation with him.

'You can't un-wish it,' the Djinn said, 'you know it's not allowed. He wanted to be young again and so he is. At least he's forgotten about his knee.'

'But he can't stay young for ever and ever,' Alan said, pushing his fingers through his hair so that it stood up in sandy spikes. 'Can he?'

'I don't think so. I suppose he'll just grow up all over again. I remember the Sultan I was telling you about, he...'

'Oh bother him,' Alan interrupted, 'what are *we* going to do?'

At that moment both boys stopped fighting as suddenly as they had begun and shook hands, panting heavily.

'You're a bonny fighter,' said Mr Grant-That-Was, 'my name's Alex and I'm pleased to know you.'

'Just you be nice to my friend, that's all,' said Johnny blowing out his cheeks. 'Well we'd better be going home and I suppose you want to get back to your hotel.'

'Hotel is it!' said Alex with a whoop of laughter, 'what hotel would that be then, I'd like to know.'

'*The* Hotel, in the middle of Sandstone,' said Lorna brushing down the boy's coat. She noticed that it was shabby and rather too small for him. Quite different from the smart suits and warm overcoats which Mr Grant usually wore.

'Oh get away,' said Alex laughing harder than ever, 'I've never been inside a hotel in my life. They're grand places and not for the likes of me.'

'Where—where do you live then?' Lorna asked.

'I dinna live onywhere,' the boy replied, putting his hands on his belt and swaggering slightly, 'I'm an orphan.'

'I *am* sorry.'

'I'm not. I'm free. I can go onywhere in the world I want. Can you keep a secret?'

'Yes,' said everybody, including the Djinn.

'I ran away from the orphanage,' Alex said, nodding in a pleased way, 'they were a right mean lot up there. And the food was something terrible and never enough of it at that.'

'Where was the orphanage?' Alan asked, with vague ideas chasing through his mind of sending Mr Grant-That-Was back to where he came from.

'Glasgie. I always wanted to run away, but I bided my time till they took me in to see about me getting a job in some factory. That's when I gave them the slip. They put me in a wee room to answer a lot of fool questions, just like school it was. It was easy to get out of there.'

'And then what did you do?' asked Alan.

'Tide's coming in,' said Johnny.

'I walked a bit and then I got a lift and then I walked a bit. I've been away now for months, they'll no be looking for me any more. I've a mind to see the world.'

He looked at their pale, starlit faces and drew himself up to his full height. He had a tough, swaggering air about him which was quite different from the anxious, fretful Mr Grant that they all knew.

'Where will you sleep tonight?' Lorna asked.

'I dinna ken,' Alex shrugged, 'under a hedge, in a haystack. What's it to you?'

Lorna exchanged glances with Alan who was biting his lip and thinking furiously.

'Tide's coming in,' Johnny said patiently.

'You'd better come home and stay with us,' Alan said, suddenly making up his mind.

'I don't know that I want to,' the boy said, with his nose in the air.

'Well we'd like you to, really we would,' Lorna said, 'and we're having welsh rarebit for supper.'

'All right,' Alex agreed with a careless shrug, 'I don't mind then, if it's what you want. Lead on.'

They set off across the rapidly narrowing sands with the boy whistling and jumping every few steps and the Djinn running and tripping as he tried to keep up. Alan had reached the conclusion that there was simply nothing he could do to improve matters at the moment. The only course of action was to hope that by some miracle they could get themselves out of their latest difficulty with the least possible trouble.

'Magic,' he grumbled to the Djinn under his breath, 'I don't know where it's all going to end.'

'Courage,' said the Djinn breathlessly, 'Mr Grant,

that is Alex, does seem happier now that he's young again.'

They were all surprised when they reached the Water Tower and put on the lights, to find out just how young he was. He had sounded quite old and grown up out on the sands, but now they saw that he was only a thin, gawky boy and that his face was tired and dirty and his clothes extremely dusty.

'I'll make you some supper now,' said Lorna, scurrying round the kitchen as fast as she could go, one eye on the loudly ticking clock on the mantelpiece, 'before my mother comes home.'

'You mean she'll not want me here?' said the boy bristling.

'Yes, no—oh don't be difficult,' Lorna snapped.

'All right, keep your hair on,' the boy replied grinning, 'this is a funny kind of house. I've never seen one like it before.'

He refused to wash his hands before he had his meal and when he did eat, it was obvious to everyone that he was very hungry indeed, for he gobbled the food up and cleaned his plate afterwards with a slice of bread.

'You're a bonny cook, girl,' he said to Lorna, pushing back his chair and stretching, 'mind you I've no doubt that any Scots girl could have done as well, but you're no bad for a Sassenach.'

Johnny looked at Alan who said wearily.

'English person. Now then Mr Gr…that is Alex, I'll show you where you can sleep.'

'Lead on,' the boy said, bowing deeply, 'I'm not tired at all mind you, but I'll have a look.'

His eyes grew a little wider when he saw Alan's bedroom, but he didn't say anything and only whistled softly as Alan and Lorna between them took a blanket and a pillow off the bed and carried them up to the tank room.

'You'll be sharing with our friend the Djinn,' said Alan, who had reached the conclusion that the only way to deal with the new Mr Grant was to tell him things very firmly.

'All right,' the boy said, 'I'm no fussy and I dinna mind sharing with *one*. After being in a dormitory with twenty-nine others it'll be like being on my own.'

'Wouldn't you like to wash?' Lorna suggested.

'I would not. Washing's girlish. I'm fine the way I am,' and he rubbed his sleeve across his dusty face, 'I'll bide up here for a while then.'

Just as they were leaving the room Alex called after Alan in a slightly softer voice.

'And I'm grateful to you.'

Alan gave him a rather strained smile and followed Lorna down the stairs. If only Alex had known that he had given up the most comfortable bedroom in the hotel for a blanket on the floor of the tank room, he might not have felt grateful at all.

'Can't leave dirty things lying about,' said Johnny, putting the table cloth absolutely straight. 'I like him.'

'You're welcome to him,' said Alan, sitting down with a thump. 'What on earth are we going to do now, have you thought of that?'

'I'm so sleepy,' said Lorna yawning, 'that I just can't bother about it at the moment.'

'I wish...' said Johnny and stopped as both his brother and sister made a lunge for him to put their hands over his mouth, 'umph, umph,' he said shaking his head furiously, 'I was only going to say,' he added very carefully, 'that it must be rather fun to run away like that. If you're an orphan.'

'Well you're not,' said Alan, sitting down again, 'so shut up. We'll have to keep him a secret until I think of what to do.'

'He liked my welsh rarebit,' said Lorna, 'I shouldn't think he'd eaten for days and days.'

'There's something I want to tell you,' said Johnny who was fidgeting round the kitchen putting things tidy.

'Not now,' said Alan crossly.

'But it's important.'

'Not NOW I said!'

Johnny snorted and went to play cat's cradle with the Djinn who whispered sympathetically.

'Your brother has much on his mind, come I will show you a new move in this game.'

Everybody was rather short-tempered and very hungry by the time they heard the vicar's old van draw up on the road and then the sound of voices.

'Quick,' said Alan, looking at the Djinn, who had got to his feet in one bound. He bowed politely and then scampered off up the stairs to reappear a moment later.

'The boy sleeps soundly, he will not wake till morning. 'Night all,' he whispered.

'He got that from Mr Antrobus,' said Alan smiling slightly as the Djinn vanished for the second time.

'I got something too,' said Johnny with a dark look at his elder brother.

'Well,' said Mrs Craig, coming in and blinking in the light, 'all safe and sound? Oh you've laid the supper, that's lovely.'

'And cooked it,' said Lorna, taking four brown and

sizzling welsh rarebits out from under the grill. 'I used rather a lot of cheese though, I hope that's all right,' she added, thinking of Alex's supper.

'Yes, yes,' Mrs Craig said absently, 'I simply must sit down for a moment.'

'I got something for you,' said Johnny.

'Have you dear? Well wait just a moment...'

'Now,' said Johnny and pulled a somewhat crumpled, sandy paper out of his pocket and handed it to her. Mrs Craig looked at it quickly and then looked again, her mouth falling open and her cheeks going so pale that Lorna rushed forward to support her.

'What is it?' Alan asked.

'A cheque,' Mrs Craig said faintly, feeling for the nearest chair and sitting down. 'A cheque for a great deal of money and it's made out to me. Johnny!' She stopped looking at the paper and grasped her son's sleeve, 'Johnny what is the meaning of this?'

'It's for the rent.'

'Yes, but,' Mrs Craig let go of him and pushed her hand across her eyes, 'yes I see dear. But we can't just accept money from people like Mr Antrobus. It's rather difficult to explain, but we just can't do it.'

'Why not?'

'I can't take presents like this from my friends,' said Mrs Craig in a shaky voice. 'It's very, very kind of him, but it's out of the question and first thing in the morning...'

'Oh is that all,' said Johnny in a relieved voice. 'It's not a present, Mum. I sold him something.'

'What?' said Mrs Craig, Alan and Lorna in one voice.

Johnny beamed at the three of them. This was his moment of triumph and he meant to make the most of it. It wasn't often that his whole family listened to what he had to say.

'Something I found on the beach,' he said happily and for a fleeting moment his eyes met Alan's. 'A bottle. So now we don't have to think about the Wicked Landlord any more do we? Can I have my supper now please? I'm hungry.'

10. *Johnny's Plan*

MRS CRAIG went off very early in the morning to see Mr Antrobus, much to everyone's relief, as it meant that Lorna was able to cook some breakfast and take it up to Alex who had slept for twelve hours without stirring, according to the Djinn.

'I'm glad you don't have to eat too,' said Lorna, drawing back the curtains.

'I'm glad I do something right,' said the Djinn sadly.

'You might have told me,' Alan was saying downstairs to Johnny who was putting all the cups the same way round on the kitchen dresser.

'Tried to. You wouldn't listen.'

'Are you sure Mr Antrobus didn't mind?' Alan asked. It was not very pleasant to discover that your younger brother is better at arranging things than you are.

'He said it was a bargain.'

'What made you think of it?'

'Alex, I mean Mr Grant-that-was. When we went to see him at the hotel after he hurt his ankle, I asked him about the bottle again, but he was all funny so I had a go at Mr Antrobus. I thought he was rich because of working such a lot. But he wasn't. So then I talked to the Djinn and we made him rich and he bought the bottle. It was easy really.'

'So that's what you were talking about yesterday,' said Alan. He made a great effort and added nobly, 'Well done, congratulations. I wish I'd thought of it.'

'Thanks,' said Johnny, going rather red and trying to pretend not to be too pleased with himself. But although it was a wonderful relief not to have to worry about the Wicked Landlord anymore, Alan was still rather out of sorts when Alex came down with Lorna and the Djinn.

'Yon fellow's a funny colour,' Alex said in a low voice to Alan.

'So are you,' Alan replied curtly. 'You'd better go and wash.'

'All right, all right. I never knew such people for soap and water.'

'We'd better go over to the hotel,' said Alan as soon as he and Lorna were alone together. 'They've probably rung up the police by now. We'll have to leave Johnny and—and him and the Djinn on their own and hope for the best.'

'But what shall we say to the hotel people?'

'I've been thinking about that. We'll say that we met Mr Grant last night—which is quite true—and that he'd had an urgent message asking him to go home, so he caught the bus to Ashford and got a train from there. He told us to give the hotel a message, but we couldn't do it till now because our mother doesn't like us being out after dark.'

'Alan you are clever,' Lorna said, which made him feel rather better.

'It's a bit thin,' he said modestly, 'but it's the best I could think of. Now I'd better have a word with Johnny.'

Johnny, who was still very full of his triumph, agreed to take the Djinn and Alex for an exploring expedition across the marsh and promised faithfully not to let anybody do any wishing if he could possibly help it.

Alan and Lorna saw them off and then made their way to Sandstone, noticing as they walked down the street that a very smart car was drawn up outside Mr Antrobus's house. They quickened their step as they didn't want their mother to see them and reached the hotel feeling rather out of breath and distinctly nervous.

The same ginger cat and the same two old ladies watched them as they walked across to the reception desk and the bored, fair-haired lady looked at them crossly and snapped:

'Well, what is it now?'

'It's about Mr Grant,' Alan said huskily. He cleared his throat. 'He gave us a message for you.'

'Oh did he indeed,' the fair-haired lady said, patting her hair. 'Very kind of him I'm sure, after the night porter stayed up till all hours to let him in.'

'He had to leave suddenly you see,' Alan went on licking his lips which had gone rather dry. It was true in a way, the real Mr Grant had left Sandstone in about thirty seconds to be exact.

'I know *that*. But where's he gone *to?*'

'Back where he came from,' Alan replied.

'Home,' Lorna added helpfully.

The fair-haired lady sniffed and looked at the large book which lay on the desk.

'I see,' she said, 'well it's a very odd way to behave I must say. It's never happened before. Oh yes, here's his address, Grace Street in Edinburgh. Well at least his account is up to date.'

'I beg your pardon?' Lorna said politely.

'He didn't owe us any money. Although there'll be the postage to pay on his clothes, still we shall have to send them cash on delivery. It's all most inconsiderate. And then there are his letters, they'll have to be forwarded too. As though I hadn't got enough to do already.'

'Yes, well,' said Alan, sliding away from the desk and feeling enormously relieved that everything had gone off so smoothly.

'There,' said the fair-haired lady, leaning over the desk and frowning more than ever, 'you've left dirty footmarks right across the carpet. You should be more careful.'

'Yes, sorry,' said Alan and fled with Lorna at his heels.

'She's about the nastiest person I've ever met,' Lorna said, 'and she's not busy at all. She didn't care at all what had happened to Alex, I mean Mr Grant. Alan what *should* we call him?'

'A dratted nuisance, look out here comes Mr Pockett.'

Mr Pockett appeared to have dressed in a hurry as he was wearing his polished gaiters with the coat of his brown winter suit. It was as though he hadn't been able to make up his mind when he got dressed, as to whether he was the aged Mr Pockett the tourists knew, or the spry Mr Pockett from the Post Office.

'Here,' he said, whacking Alan on the arm with his knobbly stick, 'I want a word with you my lad.'

'What about?'

'Come over here.' Mr Pockett drew them into a small alleyway and looked up and down it as though he expected to see somebody creeping up on them. ' 'Bout yesterday. Or to be more exact, yesterday afternoon.'

'If it's about that tea cosy, I paid the extra money,' Alan said quickly while Lorna watched him curiously.

'Ah,' said Mr Pockett, 'I had a feeling it might be something to do with you my lad. I'm not such a fool as you think.'

'I never did think you were one,' Alan said truthfully.

'Well those as do, gets a surprise. It's about this here,' and Mr Pockett took something out of his coat and held it out to them on the palm of his hand. It was round and flat and it glinted in the pale sunlight.

'It's one of the coins from the Money Tree,' Lorna said.

'One of what?' asked Mr Pockett cupping his hand round his ear. 'Speak up girl.'

Alan stared at the golden coin and suddenly everything became clear in his mind. He had meant to put his two shilling piece into the money-box yesterday, but just as he was about to do so Mr Grant–as he then was–had come up and spoken to him. So without noticing he must have put the Arabic coin in among the change instead.

'It's, it's,' Alan said desperately.

'Where did you get it, eh?' Mr Pockett asked, his eyes gleaming, his wrinkled face alive with curiosity. Alan looked at Lorna who said the first thing that came into her head.

'We–we found it,' she explained. 'Quite near the Water Tower.'

'Did you now,' Mr Pockett stroked his cheek with one bent finger. 'Daresay as how it'd been washed up then. We've had mighty high tides recently. Ah...' his eyes narrowed still further and he drew closer. 'I have heard,' he said in a hoarse whisper, 'as how you've had another find down on the sands. A little bottle worth hundreds of pounds.'

'Sixty,' Alan corrected him, 'how did you...'

'My, oh my,' Mr Pockett cackled, 'some folks has all the luck. I been combing those beaches man and boy for more years than you've had hot dinners. I never did find a thing, except a shilling or two. It's not right, so it ain't.'

'I suppose we were just lucky,' Lorna said quickly.

'Luck! Ha!' said Mr Pockett furiously and hobbled off down the alley without another backward glance.

'I suppose everybody knows about the bottle by now,' Alan said. 'Honestly if it's not one thing, it's another. I never knew what Mum meant when she said that, but I do now!'

'Never mind,' said Lorna, looking on the bright side as usual, 'at least we haven't got to worry about the Wicked Landlord any more and perhaps Mr Grant—Alex—will go off round the world and as he hasn't got a family, no one will worry. And he's not nearly as miserable now as he was when he was grown up. I wonder if we'll all get cross and worried when *we* grow up? Have you noticed how being old makes people quite different?'

'No,' said Alan, who was watching a portly young man come out of Mr Antrobus's house and who wasn't really listening.

'That fair-haired lady in the hotel's always grumbling,' said Lorna ticking people off on her fingers, 'and Mr Grant got more and more ill and funny and even Mum loses her temper sometimes. The Vicar's quite jolly, of course, but he can be snappy. But Mr Antrobus is different, he's always nice and smiling.'

'Not now he isn't,' Alan said, 'look.'

They paused in the street and watched as Mr Antrobus said goodbye to his friend. For the first time since they had known him, Mr Antrobus looked distinctly cross.

'Morning,' he said, leaning against the doorway and puffing, 'if you can call it a nice one, I can't.'

'Why?' asked Lorna.

'First it was your mother,' said Mr Antrobus sighing, 'not that I wasn't delighted to see her. Known her since she was in her pram. Well come in, come in.' He led the way through his cluttered front room and the children were surprised to see Miss Pockett there, wearing a very large apron and with her hair done up in a scarf.

'Did you ever see such a PICKLE!' Miss Pockett

demanded, 'I daresay this place hasn't had a clean out in YEARS.'

'Never wanted it,' Mr Antrobus said, quite rudely for him.

'Now, now,' said Miss Pockett waving a duster at him and Mr Antrobus grunted and led the way into the kitchen and shut the door very firmly behind him.

'Interfering,' he said. 'If there's one thing I can't stand, it's an interfering woman. Where was I?'

'Telling us that you'd known Mummy since she was a baby,' said Lorna, picking up one of the black and ginger kittens which was trying to get inside a cake tin.

'I don't mean that you mother's one of the interfering kind,' Mr Antrobus said hastily, 'but she was quite cool with me. Said she didn't want to take charity. I showed her the bottle, told her it was valuable, but she wouldn't believe me. She's gone to take it to an antique shop in Ashford if you please to get it valued by an expert. She *doubted* my word. Me, her old friend!'

'I'm sure she didn't mean to be rude,' Lorna said.

'Magic,' said Alan gloomily, 'it always mucks things up. I've noticed it before.'

'Magic?' said Mr Antrobus vaguely. 'Funny you should say that. I've been having a look through my things and I've found a whole lot more stuff. A glass ball and a whole row of little bottles, not to mention pages and pages of spells. They were all stacked away in an old wooden chest and I'd no idea I'd got them. All magic stuff. Must have belonged to an ancestor of mine. Where's that kettle?'

'Under the table,' said Alan, handing it over, 'what do you mean—magic stuff?'

'Oh potions and spells and a few poisons I shouldn't be surprised. Very interesting it all is too. Amazing what those fellows used to get up to. Searching for the elixir of youth, transmuting lead into gold, that kind of thing. Where's the tea?'

'The cat's sitting on it,' said Lorna shifting that large black creature which blinked at her sleepily and then stalked off down the draining board to sit on the tea cosy.

'Could you explain please?' Alan asked. Anything he could learn about magic might be a help.

'Well in the old days people believed in magic. They had spells for everything from making your hair curl to stopping toothache. Instead of going along to see the doctor they went and called on the local wise woman or alchemist. But what they were always searching for was the secret of giving people back their lost youth. Chuck up.'

'Sorry,' said Alan, who had coughed violently.

'And as for ways of making gold cheaply,' went on Mr Antrobus. 'The papers I found have quite a bit about that in them. I was telling that young-fellow-me-lad about it. Kettle's boiling.'

'Who was he?' asked Lorna.

'Mean to say you didn't recognise him?' said Mr Antrobus and for the first time that morning he stopped looking worried and laughed so that his face went into rubbery wrinkles. 'My word, he *would* be upset. He does that television programme, HERE AND THERE. Silly sort of show. I never watch it.'

'We haven't got a television,' Alan said rather sadly.

'Good thing too,' said Mr Antrobus, pouring out three cups of very black tea. 'There's some shortbread around somewhere. Well as I was saying–what was I saying?'

'You were talking about the young man from the television—are you going to have one?' Alan asked, while Lorna started hunting for the shortbread.

'Got one somewhere,' Mr Antrobus replied, sitting down on the creaking oak settle, 'inside a wardrobe I think. Or is that the wireless? Never mind. No, no he wants me to appear on the television.'

'Oh,' said Lorna, round-eyed with admiration, 'you'll be famous. I wish...' and then she stopped herself out of force of habit.

'Yes, I daresay,' Mr Antrobus said doubtfully, 'but the truth of the matter is I don't like people staring at me. I look funny I know...'

'No you don't,' Lorna said and added, 'I've found the shortbread.'

'Yes I do,' Mr Antrobus said firmly, taking a handful of biscuits. 'Always have and always will. That's why I can't stand it when the holiday people come round in the summer and start gaping at me, so I stare back at *them* and that scares 'em off. Anyway this television chap kept on nagging at me, so in the end I agreed.'

'Well I think it's marvellous,' said Lorna, her eyes watering as she sipped at the strong black tea. 'Why does he want you to be on it though?'

'It's those articles I'm writing,' Mr Antrobus said. 'Caused quite a stir they have. And the moment I did agree, that chap started turning the place upside down to see where he could put his cameras. That's when she turned up.' And he nodded gloomily towards the front room where they could hear Miss Pockett moving furniture about.

'There's a whole lot of 'em coming down to do the

programme,' Mr Antrobus went on, dipping a biscuit in his tea, 'and this chap said there wasn't enough room to swing a cat in the parlour—lot of nonsense—as though anybody ever wanted to swing a cat—would they my beauty, eh?'

The black cat turned round three times and sat down again on the cosy, sharpening her claws on the draining board.

'Where was I?' said Mr Antrobus. 'Oh yes, so before I knew what was happening Alice Pockett was on the doorstep—just like her father she is, knows when something's up before anybody else so much as gets a sniff of it—asking if I wanted some clearing up done. And this young chap hauls her inside and in no time flat she's turning the whole place upside down.'

'Well,' said Alan as Mr Antrobus paused for breath.

'Won't you like being famous?' Lorna asked. She would have loved to have been famous herself and she had often imagined how wonderful it would be to appear on television.

'No,' said Mr Antrobus flatly, 'I shall hate it. Funny thing you know I always wanted to write something which'd make people sit up and take notice. I thought it'd be nice to be famous and rich, but the truth of the matter is I was happier before it all happened. I liked pottering about in my own good time doing what *I* wanted without a lot of bossy, interfering people running my life for me. I wish I could get away from it all.'

'Can't you?' said Alan, who was starting to feel that the sugary shortbread was turning into sawdust in his mouth.

'I dunno,' Mr Antrobus said vaguely. 'Although that

friend of yours did put an idea into my head. I liked him, interesting chap.'

'Mr Chinn?' said Lorna. 'What—what idea was that?'

'Going abroad,' said Mr Antrobus, finishing up the biscuits and licking his fingers. 'Supposing I upped sticks and went off to Arabia?'

11. *Treasure Hunt*

'It's aye too flat for me,' said Alex, gazing across the rippling marsh. 'I like a few mountains myself.'

'Do you have mountains in Glasgow?' asked Johnny.

They had been for a very long walk and although the two boys were quite fresh, the Djinn was looking tired so they had sat down under the lee of a sandbank for the wind was getting up and the sea was full of white horses.

'Och no,' Alex replied, watching a seagull float past on a current of air. 'But I mind one summer when we spent ten days in camp up on the north coast near a wee place called Tongue. It was bonny up there all right. There were rabbits and sheep and deer and one night we nearly caught a stag. He was a fine fellow, he came trotting down the road as though he owned the place, tame as you please, but proud with it.'

'We've got sheep and rabbits on the marsh,' Johnny said, 'and there's lobsters and crabs and fishes and...'

'So have we,' Alex said at once, 'bigger than yours too I bet.'

'When I was here before,' said the Djinn, who didn't want them to start fighting again, 'all this was part of the sea.'

'I dinna believe that,' said Alex.

'I do,' said Johnny.

'It's true enough,' the Djinn replied, taking off one sandal and shaking out the sand. Alex looked curiously at his green toes and the Djinn went on, 'Sea it was, right up as far as Tenterden and Rye, why they used to sail big boats up there. There were shipyards building galleons there, my master told me so.'

'But what happened to the sea, where did it go?' asked Johnny, wondering if somewhere in the world somebody had pulled out an enormous plug and drained away some of the oceans.

'They started draining the marsh,' the Djinn replied, getting to work on the second sandal. 'Some men came from the Low Countries across the Channel and showed how it could be done. Round here it was all little islands in those days. Surely you've heard of the Isle of Thanet?'

'Where Ramsgate and Broadstairs and Margate are?' asked Johnny, 'but that's all Kent, it's just *called* an isle.'

'Because it was one once, that's why,' the Djinn said simply.

'Here,' said Alex, who had been thinking hard, 'when would this have been?'

'Three to four hundred years ago,' the Djinn replied.

'Then how can you remember it?'

'Because I'm older even than that,' the Djinn replied with pride. 'Look, here comes the aged and venerable gentleman who sold us the ring of my master.'

'Mr Pockett?' said Johnny, peering round the edge of the dune. A small figure with a flapping overcoat was moving slowly along the edge of the rippling surf with his eyes fixed on the sands, but in spite of this he noticed the boys and the Djinn almost at once.

'Hi,' said Mr Pockett, his voice nearly lost in the high-spirited wind, 'I've been hoping I'd see you. Come over here.'

The flying spray and the clouds of fine sand made their eyes water and their cheeks smart as they went across to join him and Mr Pockett, leaning against the wind as though it were a comfortable armchair, took out his handkerchief and rubbed his face with it.

'Dratted stuff,' he muttered, 'gets into everything, it do. Well now, I seen your brother and sister a while back and they told me you'd show me where you found that little coin from Araby, so they did.'

Johnny's eyes grew round with surprise and he stared at Mr Pockett who looked blandly back at him.

'Well get a move on then,' said Mr Pockett, 'haven't got all day. We've had to shut the Post Office for the morning as it is, what with me daughter jauntering off to Mr Antrobus's and me with other things on me mind. Show us then.'

Johnny appealed mutely to the Djinn who looked as perplexed as he did and Mr Pockett said testily.

'So that's how it is, is it? You want to keep it all to yourselves. You never think what a few comforts might mean to a poor old man like me. What'll happen to me if they throws me out of my cottage? I'll be out in the street that's what! And no where to go 'cause I haven't got but a few pounds put by which 'as taken me all me life to save.'

As Johnny was now completely bewildered he kept quiet. It seemed very unlikely that Alan or Lorna would have told Mr Pockett about the Money Tree and yet, in his mysterious way, he seemed to know all about it. Why he should have to leave his cottage or what that had to do with it, Johnny had not the least idea.

'Away with you,' said Alex, 'you're trying it on.'

'And who are you when you're at home?' demanded Mr Pockett, 'go back to Ireland where you come from.'

'Scotland!' said Alex, going pale with fury.

'You'm all furriners,' said Mr Pockett, 'same as him,' and he nodded at the Djinn. He had worked himself up into a thoroughly bad temper, for he'd had a very tiring morning looking for gold coins and he hadn't found a thing.

'Why do you want to look for Arabian money?'

Johnny asked. 'It's not real you know, you can't buy anything with it. Alan said so.'

'Cause it's pretty,' said Mr Pockett, 'and I likes pretty things about me. If I has to leave my cottage and go into one of them Homes, at least I'd have my pretty coins to look at. T'int much to ásk,' and he dabbed his eyes.

'A Home?' said Alex. 'Is that like an orphanage?'

'So t'is, only worse,' said Mr Pockett with such an enormous sigh that he rose up on his toes and nearly lost his balance.

'Then I'm sorry if I was rude,' said Alex. 'When I'm a grown man I'd like to build houses for people, not turn them out of them. I never thought of it before, but it's what I'd like to do.'

'Ah, I daresay,' said Mr Pockett, 'but I can't wait that long, can I? I did think Johnny my old friend'd do what he could to help. But then I suppose I'm old enough to realise that it's when the hard times come that you find out who your real friends are.'

Johnny saw the Djinn and Alex looking at him sadly and he said furiously.

'Well it's not MY fault. I wish you could find the beastly gold money if you want it so badly, but—oh!'

There was an extra strong gust of wind at that moment and as the Djinn shivered, far out to sea a great current whirled round the Money Tree where it stood on the ocean floor and the gold pieces were torn off the branches like blossom blown by the wind. They scattered through the water, a shoal of spinning golden coins and were carried on and on, dancing and glittering towards the shore, and as Mr Pockett turned mournfully in the direction of Sandstone a great grey wave came churning and leaping across the sea and then with a thundering roar it leapt into the air, dissolved into spray and threw itself on the sand.

'My word, that was a big 'un,' said Mr Pockett, dancing back nimbly as the edges of the spray came right up to his feet in frothing, lacy patterns.

'Tidal wave,' said Johnny. 'Bet it's rougher than you get it in Scotland.'

'We have them twice as big,' said Alex, 'sometimes THREE times as big.'

'How I dislike the sea,' the Djinn murmured to himself.

'Oh, oh, oh,' shouted Mr Pockett, 'look at that, oh my, oh my, oh my!'

For there, still in the shape of the retreating ripples were row after row of golden coins. Everybody stared at them and Alex rubbed his knuckles in his eyes and the Djinn hummed softly to himself. Johnny swallowed several times and Mr Pockett, coming to his senses first, made a grab at the small bucket which Johnny had brought along for crabs.

'Give us that boy,' he said, 'and give us a hand too. But mind—I saw 'em first. Come on, don't dilly-dally or there'll be another wave and I'll have lost the lot.'

'There won't,' said Johnny, but Mr Pockett was already down on his hands and knees shovelling up the gold pieces as fast as he could go.

When it was full the bucket was so heavy that it took all four of them to lift it. Mr Pockett, who kept giving a little jump every few steps, insisted on tucking his handkerchief over the top for, as he said several times, he didn't want any nosey-parkers sticking their noses into his affairs. Although the wind was behind them it was a very long and tiring journey and Mr Pockett didn't even bother to say thank you when they reached his cottage and put the bucket on the table.

'My bucket,' said Johnny as Mr Pockett pushed them all out of the door.

'Later,' said Mr Pockett. 'Not now boy. Go on, off.' And he slammed the door behind them and they heard the bolts rattle into position.

'Oh let's go then,' said Johnny crossly. Several people were looking curiously at the Djinn who, what with the wind and the exercise had a high colour in his cheeks so that they were a deep, moss green. Johnny stumped off feeling very hurt at the way Mr Pockett had behaved and he didn't even notice a large poster which had been pinned up in the Post Office window underneath the closed sign.

'Never mind,' said Lorna, when she heard the whole story back at the Water Tower. 'Let's have lunch and then you'll feel better.'

'I don't feel bad now,' said Johnny with a face like thunder and stamped up to the tank room.

'It's a bit early for lunch isn't it?' asked Alan, who had been thinking deeply.

'Not really,' said Lorna, who was longing to start cooking, 'and as Mum's gone to Ashford for the day she's left us our lunch to heat up. We can all have it together.'

'I'll give you a hand,' said Alex and actually went and washed under the kitchen tap without being asked.

'It's a funny thing,' Alan said, 'but money seems to make people miserable or bad-tempered. Mr You-Know-Who must have been jolly rich staying in the best bedroom at the hotel, but he was always sad. Now Mr Antrobus has got rich, he's not cheerful any more and now Mr Pockett's going funny.'

'Well he won't be able to spend his money,' Lorna said, lighting the oven with a flourish and putting in the macaroni cheese, 'it's not worth anything after all because it's foreign.'

But there she proved to be quite mistaken, for in that mysterious way in which news got about in Sandstone, everybody seemed to know about Mr Pockett's find in no time at all and everybody said that Mr Pockett was now a very rich man.

'But he can't be,' objected Lorna, when the postman stopped at the Water Tower and told her the news.

'It's true right enough,' the postman said, handing over a letter, 'they say there's some antiquing chap come across from Ashford specially to value the coins and he says they're worth a fortune. As soon as I've finished my rounds I'm off to the beach myself.'

'What for?' asked Alan.

'Why to look for gold of course. Half the shops in the town's closed this morning and the hardware's sold clean out of buckets and shovels. Everybody's down on the sands digging for all they're worth. I won't stop for a cup of tea today, thanks all the same. I haven't the time.'

And he went off and rode his bicycle down the bumpy road faster than anybody had ever seen him do it before.

'I *told* you my Money Tree was a good idea,' said Johnny, sitting half-way down the stairs and tying his shoe-laces into neat bows, 'but you wouldn't listen.'

'It's not fair,' Lorna said, her mouth trembling, 'it's ours.'

'Not any more it isn't,' Alan said heavily.

'And it took me all that time to work out how to make Mr Antrobus rich so he'd buy the Djinn's bottle,' said Johnny, mulling over his grievance. 'Where is the Djinn anyway?'

'Gone for a walk,' Alan said, 'but come to that, where's Alex?'

'Isn't he in the tank room?' Lorna asked.

'No, I looked up there just before the postman came,' Alan said, starting to feel thoroughly alarmed. Now that the problem of the Wicked Landlord had been dealt with—at least for the present—there were still the problems of turning Alex back into Mr Grant and getting the Djinn to Arabia to be tackled. It seemed that no sooner had they got over one difficulty than more cropped up to take its place.

'You're both looking very thoughtful,' said Mrs Craig coming into the kitchen. 'Come along now breakfast time. Isn't it extraordinary about old Mr Pockett? I've just been down on the beach for a breath of air and the sands are covered with people, all digging like mad things. The Vicar was walking up and down trying to talk to them, but nobody would listen. In fact one or two of them were quite rude to him. He looked so upset, poor man. Then Mr Antrobus arrived in the most splendid car with that young man from the television. He started digging too.'

'Not Mr Antrobus?' said Alan, trying to imagine that large and portly gentleman doing anything so strenuous.

'Oh no,' Mrs Craig said smiling, 'he went over to talk to the Vicar and they went off shaking their heads.

I meant the television man, he'd got a shovel in the boot of his car.'

A feeling of great uneasiness descended on Alan and Lorna. It was all because of them that this was happening and Alan, for one, was sure that no good would come of it. They hadn't meant any harm to anyone, all they had wanted to do was to confound the Wicked Landlord and help the Djinn into the bargain, but one thing had led to another with alarming speed and goodness knew where it all was going to end.

'He's not there,' said Johnny, coming down the stairs from the tank room with a rush.

'Who dear?' said Mrs Craig opening her letter.

But Johnny, who never answered questions if they had difficult answers, only smiled vaguely and helped himself to cereal.

'Both of them gone,' Alan whispered to Lorna, 'but where?'

Lorna shook her head and then glanced at her mother who was staring at the letter with all the colour leaving her cheeks.

'What is it?' asked Alan, his voice sharp with agitation.

'It's, it's the Wicked Landlord,' Mrs Craig said huskily, 'that is Mr Blofelt. They're going to buy up the Water Tower.'

'But they can't—it's ours.'

'No it isn't, we just rent it from them. Apparently they've a big plan to buy up property all over the district because they want to redevelop the area.'

'I don't understand,' said Johnny.

'It means,' said Mrs Craig slowly, 'that they're going to knock down a lot of houses—including the tower—so as to build new ones in their place.'

'So *that's* what Mr Pockett meant,' said Johnny, glad to have one mystery solved.

'But they can't,' Lorna wailed, 'not after everything we've done.'

'They can,' said Mrs Craig, trying to smile, 'and I'm very much afraid that there's nothing we can do to stop them!'

12. *Alan Makes a Discovery*

'No hawkers, no travellers,' said Miss Pockett, trying to shut the door. 'Please go away because I'm very BUSY.'

'Please, honourable and distinguished lady,' said the Djinn bowing deeply, 'this is of great importance.'

'Yes, I dare say,' said Miss Pockett, folding her arms, 'and if it's RUGS you're selling, we've got more than enough of THEM already.'

'If you could just enquire of your learned master,' the Djinn said, 'whether he'll have the gracious goodness to see us, that is all I ask.'

'Ay, go on missus,' said Alex, 'it canna do any harm.'

'Well I would if I COULD,' said Miss Pockett, softening a little, 'but I can't. He's gone down to the beach along with the rest of the people in this town, so he's NOT at home. Good morning.'

And this time she did manage to shut the door leaving Alex and the Djinn on the outside. The Djinn hitched up his coat and sighed gently and Alex patted him on the shoulder and said:

'Cheer up. It's not the end of the world.'

'It's going to be the end of my world,' said the Djinn, 'all I have tried to do to help has ended in disaster. I did my best, but it was not enough and they have been so good to me. So kind, so patient, never a word of reproach.'

'Pull yourself together, man,' Alex said sternly.

'I'm *not* a man, I'm a Djinn, that's the point.'

'Ay, I was forgetting. Well let's bide here a wee while longer. Yon Mr Antrobus can't stay away from his own house for ever, although it's a funny looking place right enough.'

But the Djinn was in no mood to be cheered up. For the last few days he had been growing steadily sadder and sadder and the previous night he had suddenly unburdened himself to Alex. Alex had listened with his eyes growing larger and larger while the Djinn told him the whole story—although he felt it wiser to leave out the bit about Alex really being middle-aged Mr Grant.

'It's a great tale,' Alex said at the finish, 'but now they've got the money from your bottle there's no more to worry about.'

'Oh but there is,' the Djinn replied, twisting his fingers into knots, 'I made a man vanish for one thing and for another I put a spell on their Wicked Landlord and for some time I've known at the back of my mind that *that's* gone wrong. If there was only somebody wise and learned to whom I could take my troubles. I remember when I was in the desert there was this sheik who wished for all his neighbours goats to turn pink. Well I managed that all right, but the trouble was I'd made it catching so all my master's goats went pink too. I had to call on one of the Mighty Djinns to aid me, but there aren't any in Kent!'

'There's yon Mr Antrobus,' Alex said slowly, 'Johnny's always talking about how clever he is.'

'Yes,' the Djinn agreed, 'I rather liked him too. He made me think of the happy past. I wonder...' He wondered for so long that Alex dozed off and he jumped violently when the Djinn suddenly shook him awake.

'I have a plan,' the Djinn whispered, his eyes blazing like emeralds, 'if you will help me?'

'I'll do what I can,' Alex said yawning. 'Yon Craigs have been good to me too, even if they do hide me away up here. Now let me get some sleep or I'll not have a clear head in the morning.'

Alex was thinking about this midnight conversation when the door opened and Miss Pockett came out wearing her hat and coat. She sniffed when she saw that they were still waiting and then hurried off down the empty street towards the Church Hall. A few minutes later Mr Antrobus's large shape came into sight moving very slowly with the tall Vicar by his side. Alex and the Djinn drew back into the alley and as the Vicar went past they heard him say:

'Yes, yes a Mr Blofelt. He wrote saying he wanted to hire the hall for his meeting and I could hardly refuse. Although if anyone will attend with all this mad hunting going on, I don't know. It's a sad business Antrobus. Greed does dreaful things to the human soul.'

'Umph,' said Mr Antrobus, 'you're right there. I shall be glad when everything gets back to normal. What with that confounded editor ringing me up every half-hour and that fellow from the TV breathing down my neck, not to mention Alice Pockett turning the house upside down, my life isn't worth living. Sure you won't stop for some coffee?'

'No, I thank you. I must hurry on my way to put out the chairs for the meeting. Good day Antrobus.'

Mr Antrobus was about to shut his front door when Alex and the Djinn appeared before him. He looked at them vaguely and then smiled as he recognised his friend from Arabia.

'What, not down on the beach?' he said, 'well come in, come in.'

To anybody who knew Mr Antrobus well his front room would have been something of a surprise, for it was extremely neat and tidy, although very over-furnished, and it smelt strongly of polish.

'Horrible isn't it?' said Mr Antrobus gloomily, 'I can't find anything. My dear sir, are you feeling unwell?' For the Djinn had just uttered a high pitched shriek and was sinking on to his knees, his hands stretched out before him.

'Get up,' Alex said, tugging at him.

But the Djinn went on bowing up and down, muttering and mumbling under his breath. Mr Antrobus watched him with mild interest and then squeezed his way round the furniture to see what had caused the Djinn's unusual behaviour.

'Dear me,' he said, panting slightly, 'it's that old picture is it? I must admit it gave me quite a turn when I first saw it too. Miss Pockett found it in the back of that old chest where all the papers and diaries were. Ugly looking chap isn't he? Rather like me except that he's got a two foot beard.'

Alex cleared his throat and peered at the dark oil painting which stared out across the crowded room. It was so dirty he could hardly see it properly but he could just make out a very round, fat, pale face with a rubbery nose and a shiny bald head.

'Ay,' Alex agreed, 'it is very much like you, sir.'

'Oh honourable one, oh my master,' said the Djinn, still bowing, 'it is indeed you. In the portrait you have a beard, that is why I did not at first recognise you. Forgive me.'

'Now what's he talking about?' asked Mr Antrobus.

'The ring,' said the Djinn, taking it out of his pocket and handing it up to Mr Antrobus, 'it came from this house did it not, oh wise one?'

'So it did yes,' agreed Mr Antrobus, 'I gave it to old Pockett for his jumble stall. But forgive me, I still don't quite see...Would you like some coffee my boy? By the way what is your name?'

'Alex. Ay, I would please sir.'

'Stay,' the Djinn implored Mr Antrobus, clutching at his hand, 'tell me first, how did you come to this house?'

'Left to me by a great-aunt,' said Mr Antrobus, 'been

in the family for years I believe. Nearly got burnt down once so I was told, that's why it's such a funny shape. The next Antrobus just built on another bit.'

'Then,' said the Djinn, lying flat on the floor, 'you are indeed the descendant of my great and good master and I salaam before you.'

'Very nice of you,' said Mr Antrobus, 'only I'd get up if I were you, it's draughty down there. Can't say I quite follow what you're on about, but it sounds interesting. I wonder where that Pockett put my kettle. Used to keep it in the stove.'

'On the stove, sir,' Alex said helpfully.

'Silly sort of place to put a kettle,' Mr Antrobus said. 'Light the gas, there's a good chap. Now then, Mr Chinn isn't it? Tell me some more about this ancestor of mine if you'd be so kind. I must say I've been getting very interested in him ever since I found his diaries. Been thinking actually,' Mr Antrobus lowered himself on the settle carefully, 'that I might write his life history. I believe he travelled a lot, even went to Arabia. I'd like to follow in his footsteps, but really I'm too old. Still I wish I could.'

The Djinn quivered and glanced imploringly at Alex just as somebody knocked on the front door.

'What did you say sir?' asked Alex.

'Said I wished I could go to Arabia,' said Mr Antrobus, wheezing at the very idea. The Djinn shivered and held his breath and muttered and Mr Antrobus added, 'well and why shouldn't I, come to that! I've got the money now, so I could do it in comfort. Yes, by George I *will* go as soon as this television business is over. See who's at the door would you Alex?'

It was Alan, Lorna and Johnny all rather breathless

and anxious looking, but their faces cleared a little when they saw Alex and beyond him the Djinn, who was gazing at Mr Antrobus with an expression of dog-like devotion.

'You might have left a note, telling us where you'd gone,' Alan said in an angry whisper.

'Och, dinna upset yourself. We're all right, in fact we're just fine. Anyway I didn't know we were going to be away so long. What's the matter with you?'

In quick, breathless voices they told him about the letter from the Wicked Landlord.

'It's no good,' Alan said at the end, 'you wouldn't understand anyway, but something's gone wrong somewhere and now we're worse off than when we started.'

'Mum's awfully upset,' Lorna said in a shaky voice, 'everything's horrid and I hate it.'

'The people are coming back from the beach,' said Johnny, 'they do look cross, I suppose it's because they didn't find anything. I tried to tell the postman it wasn't any good, but he just shouted at me to go away. He was as nasty as Mr Pockett.'

'Dear me, dear me,' said Mr Antrobus looming up in the doorway, 'so you've heard about the redevelopment plan. There have been rumours flying about for some time and yesterday there was a notice up about it in the Post Office. The Vicar told me this morning that a Mr Blofelt from the Property Company concerned was coming down to address a meeting in the Church Hall. I shouldn't go if I were you. Only upset yourselves.'

'The Wicked Landlord—here!' said Alan.

'At the hotel I believe,' said Mr Antrobus, 'won't you have some coffee? The kettle is boiling.' It was screaming in its high-pitched way out in the kitchen while the Djinn eyed it nervously.

'Can't stop, thank you,' said Alan, making up his mind quickly. 'Please could our friend Mr Chinn come too?'

'We were having rather an interesting discussion,' Mr Antrobus said and then, seeing how anxious Alan was looking he added kindly, 'still I daresay it'll keep. Mr Chinn?'

The Djinn with a wide smile on his face came floating out to join them and although Alan was moving from foot to foot with impatience, the Djinn insisted on bowing ceremoniously to Mr Antrobus before he would leave.

'But what good will it do, going to see the Wicked Landlord?' asked Lorna, as they half-ran, half-walked towards the hotel.

'I don't know, but we've got to stop him somehow. He's not going to take the Water Tower away from us and that's flat. Come on and don't argue.'

The two old ladies and the fat ginger cat were all sitting up very straight, trying to overhear what the cross fair-haired lady at the desk was saying to a thin, very smart gentleman who was with her. She glanced up when the children came into the foyer and her expression grew even crosser.

'I've got no time for you now,' she said.

'We want to see Mr Blofelt,' said Alan.

'That's me,' said the gentleman, 'and if it's about the redevelopment scheme, you can put your questions at the proper place and time.'

Alan, Lorna and Johnny hardly heard what he was saying, because they all felt rather strange at coming face to face with the Wicked Landlord after all this time. He wasn't at all like they had imagined him to be, he looked just like anybody else only richer, and it was a bit of a let-down.

'Well,' he said turning back to the fair-haired lady, 'it's all most extraordinary. Of course, he was on the verge of a nervous breakdown, that's why he dropped everything and came here for a rest. He certainly never returned to the office. Are you certain that you got the address right? He must have sent us some kind of message.'

'He didn't leave any message at all, sir,' the fair-haired lady said stiffly, 'of course if you doubt my word...'

'Please,' said Alan tugging at Mr Blofelt's arm.

'Go away,' Mr Blofelt said irritably.

'I'll call the porter,' the fair-haired lady said.

'Come on,' whispered Lorna, 'everybody's staring.'

'No,' said Alan, going very red, but standing his ground.

'I'll deal with you in a minute,' said the fair-haired lady. 'Now then sir,' and she picked up the big book on the desk and turned it round so that he could read it. 'That's the address *we* have, Grace Street, Edinburgh.'

'It looks like a matter for the police,' said Mr Blofelt. 'A man can't just vanish. Particularly an important man who's Chairman of a large company.'

'What's Chairman?' said Johnny.

'The head person,' said Alan.

'But,' said Johnny and stopped.

'Porter,' called the fair-haired lady, 'Porter, come and escort these children out of here.'

The porter came slowly across the foyer and Alan after one desperate look at Mr Blofelt, slowly backed away across the floor.

'Shame,' said one of the old ladies, 'they're only children.'

'That was his name down the side of the letter,' said Johnny, who like Alan was retreating backwards. 'The letter Mum had that first time. It said Chairman at the top. I thought it was funny the Benovlent people making chairs.'

'Grace Street,' said Alan.

'Out,' said the Porter pushing them through the swing doors and out into the street.

'It looks a grand place,' said Alex, who was hanging about on the corner, hunching his shabby coat against the wind off the sea. 'I thought you'd come here. Man, but you look strange!'

Alan gaped at him, his mind going round and round in circles and then with a hand that trembled he took hold of Alex's arm and said in a thick, husky voice:

'It's you. YOU'RE THE WICKED LANDLORD!'

13. *The Meeting*

'BUT I don't want to be a grown up,' Alex said stubbornly, 'I like it fine the way I am.'

The five of them were huddled in the little alley, keeping out of sight of the people who were all streaming towards the Church Hall. Most of them looked angry and they all had very sandy shoes.

'But you don't want us to be turned out of the Water Tower do you?' asked Lorna.

'No,' Alex admitted, 'but I don't want to be old either.'

'If you ask me,' said the Djinn, in his soft voice, 'that Mr Blofelt's the one who's behind all this. I think he's been planning it all while Alex was away ill, he looks that kind of person from the glimpse I had. We had a Grand Vizier once who tried to seize power while the Sheik was away. His eyes were very close together too.'

'Please,' Lorna said, 'please help us.'

Alex looked at their anxious faces and remembered how they had helped him. He heaved an enormous sigh and straightened his shoulders.

'Och, very well,' he said slowly, 'but what is it I have to do?'

'Ah,' said the Djinn, rubbing his hands together, 'now if you'll kindly listen to me I think I see how it can be done. There's one good thing anyway, everybody's in such a bad temper because they didn't find any coins, that they'll be in just the right mood to make trouble. Now then, this is what we'll do...'

The village hall was very full and already rather stuffy as Lorna and Johnny joined their mother in the back row. Mr Antrobus had kept seats for them and he smiled and nodded as they sat down.

'Don't you worry my dear,' he said patting Mrs Craig's hand, 'you haven't lost your Water Tower yet.'

Mrs Craig smiled faintly and then turned to Lorna and said, 'Where's Alan? I thought he was with you.'

'He, he saw a friend outside,' said Lorna, who's face

was scarlet with excitement and heat. 'He'll be here in a minute,' and she crossed her fingers and took hold of Johnny's arm for comfort.

The Vicar climbed up onto the platform followed by Mr Blofelt and from several parts of the hall there was the sound of muffled booing.

'My friends,' said the Vicar, 'I should like you to meet Mr Blofelt of the Benevolent...'

'Take my cottage away from me would you?' called out Mr Pockett who was wearing his gaiters and moleskin jacket, 'take away the roof from over a poor man's defenceless head.'

There was a burst of laughter from one side of the hall and Mr Pockett turned and glared in that direction. The laughter died away and it grew so quiet you could hear the sound of people breathing.

'Now, now Mr Pockett,' said the Vicar, 'all in good time. Everyone can state their case later.'

'I'm stating mine *now*,' said Mr Pockett.

'It's downright wicked and DISGRACEFUL,' said Miss Pockett, coming to her father's assistance, 'you ought to be ashamed of yourself.'

Mr Blofelt smiled thinly and the fair-haired lady from the hotel turned round and said:

'Oh be quiet all of you.'

'S'all right for you,' shouted Mr Pockett, thumping on the chair in front of him with his stick, 'you'm a furriner, you don't belong here. T'int your house they're a-going to knock down.'

'I am NOT a foreigner,' said the fair-haired lady getting up, 'I was born and bred in Rye, let me tell you.'

'See—a furriner,' said Mr Pockett triumphantly and sat down to a round of applause.

'Ladies, gentlemen,' said the Vicar, waving his arms up and down, 'please, please let Mr Blofelt speak. Let us hear his side.'

'He hasn't got a side,' said Mr Antrobus, suddenly entering the discussion. He got to his feet with the help of Mrs Craig. 'This is a happy, friendly community. We're perfectly satisfied as we are. We don't want to be rehoused and replanned and ordered about. At least I don't for one and there are plenty more like me.'

'Here, here,' shouted the postman.

'And what's more,' went on Mr Antrobus warming to his subject, 'I shall say so when I go on the televison.'

There was an outbreak of cheering at this and Mr Antrobus sat down again with a thump which made Lorna's chair shake.

The Vicar turned and said something in a low voice to Mr Blofelt who by this time was looking extremely angry. He got to his feet and the booing started again and then Mr Pockett began to clap his hands together very slowly and everybody else started to do the same.

'Ladies and gentlemen,' shouted Mr Blofelt above the din, 'I can assure you that our plan will bring even greater happiness and prosperity to your lovely town and what is more...'

'Sit down, we don't want none of your plans,' roared Mr Pockett, who had a surprisingly loud voice for someone so old.

'Order, order,' called the Vicar, banging on the table.

'Go on, go on,' Johnny said, pushing at Lorna.

'I can't, I can't. My heart's banging and my hands are all sweaty. I CAN'T'.

'Then I will,' said Johnny and stood up. As he was

not a great deal taller standing up than he was when was sitting down, nobody took any notice, so Johnny carefully climbed up on to his chair.

'Johnny darling get down,' said Mrs Craig.

'No,' said Johnny, 'not yet.' He cleared his throat and then bellowed at the top of his voice. 'You're a Wicked Landlord.'

The clapping and the booing died away and everybody turned round and an awful silence descended on the stuffy hall. Johnny stared straight ahead and ignored his mother who was tugging at his elbow.

'I say, steady on,' Mr Antrobus said quietly.

'You're a Wicked Landlord,' Johnny shouted again.

'I am nothing of the kind,' Mr Blofelt said furiously, 'I am merely the Secretary of the Association, but I have the full authorisation of...'

'What's authorisation?' asked Johnny.

'Power,' whispered Mr Antrobus.

'Authorisation of the Chairman to act in his absence,' said Mr Blofelt gathering speed.

'Where is the Chairman?' shouted Johnny.

'I don't know,' said Mr Blofelt before he could stop himself. 'That is, he's on holiday.'

'That's right,' agreed the fair-haired lady, 'he was staying in our hotel. He disappeared a few days ago.'

'What have you done with him?' demanded Johnny. The whispers which had started up at the word 'disappeared' stopped and Mr Blofelt suddenly found that everybody in the Hall was staring at him in the most frightening and unnerving manner.

'I haven't done anything with him,' he said, mopping his forehead with a silk handkerchief. 'In fact I came down here to find him, but this has nothing to do with the present situation.'

'It has,' argued Johnny, 'he's a nice kind man. He wouldn't turn people out. He told me so.'

'I only wish he was here then,' said Mr Antrobus, 'but really Johnny as he isn't...'

'Exactly,' said Mr Blofelt. 'Little boy sit down at once.'

There was a slight commotion at the back of the hall and the Djinn, who had been standing just outside with Alan, stopped muttering and shivering and a rather surprised and dazed looking Mr Grant suddenly appeared in the doorway.

'Remember,' Alan whispered fiercely, 'remember everything we told you.'

Mr Grant looked at him for one fleeting moment with the eyes of Alex, and then he shook his head in a rather bewildered manner and then walked purposefully down the aisle with his overcoat flapping behind him.

'Mr Grant,' said Mr Blofelt, his eyes bulging. 'Why —why this is a surprise.'

'So it seems,' said Mr Grant grimly, 'a surprise for both of us. Now then everybody, I am the Chairman of the Association and I should like to say a few words if you'll be so kind as to listen to me.'

Johnny climbed down off his chair, his legs shaking so much he had to put his hands on his knees to steady them.

'Oh, you *were* brave,' Lorna said.

'Making a spectacle of yourself like that,' said Mrs Craig. 'Really Johnny, I don't know what came over you.'

'I thought it was a pretty good effort myself,' said Mr Antrobus winking at him, 'have a toffee, you look as though you could do with one.'

Mr Grant held up his hands for silence and began to make his speech. It was quite a short one, but it was what everybody wanted to hear, for he said that while he was getting over an illness, matters at his office appeared to have got rather out of hand. He had no plans to redevelop the area or to turn anybody out.

There was a tremendous burst of cheering and Mr Blofelt seemed to slide further and further back in his chair.

'You know,' said Mr Grant, leaning forward and smiling and not looking anything like anybody's idea of a Wicked Landlord, 'I came down here for rest and quiet and I found them. At first I didn't enjoy my stay, unfortunately, as I had a series of small accidents.'

Johnny and Lorna exchanged guilty glances and then stared straight ahead again.

'And then,' Mr Grant went on, 'I started to recall the days of my youth and the plans I had made then. The idealistic plans of youth perhaps, but just because we grow older is there any reason why we should forget our dreams?'

Outside, the Djinn and Alan looked at one another and the Djinn wiped beads of cold green sweat off his forehead.

'A close thing,' he said. 'If Mr Antrobus hadn't wished...'

'Well he did,' Alan said feeling quite sick with relief. 'Do you realise that it was *us* who made all those awful things happen to Mr Grant?'

'I had a few faint suspicions,' the Djinn said, nodding, 'that time when he was chased by the wild dog for one. I'd seen a dog like that before in the desert. I remember there was this Arab trader who was always giving short measure...'

'It's a pity Alex has gone,' Alan said sighing, 'and I should have noticed Mr Grant's name on that letter and worked it all out long ago.'

'You had a great deal on your mind,' the Djinn said gently. There was a thunderous roar from inside the hall and then a few moments later the door was thrown open and people started pouring out headed by Mr Antrobus and Mrs Craig.

'Alan,' she said, so excited that she completely failed to notice the Djinn who had flattened himself against the wall. 'You missed it all! Guess what, it was Mr, Grant who was the—the landlord and he's going to let me keep the Water Tower at the old rent. I can hardly believe it, oh dear I do believe I'm going to cry.'

'Don't,' said Lorna. 'Please don't.'

There was the sound of more cheering from inside the Hall and then somebody started singing, "For He's A Jolly Good Fellow" and everybody else joined in.

'Well I don't know I'm sure,' said the fair-haired lady from the hotel pushing past Miss Pockett, 'I thought it'd do this town some good, put a bit of life into it.'

'Oh I do wish she'd be nice,' said Lorna, 'she's always so cross and she spoils everything.'

The Djinn, sheltering behind the door, cast up his emerald eyes and held his breath and the fair-haired lady suddenly stopped pushing and turned round and actually smiled at Mrs Craig. It made her look much prettier.

'Still,' she said, 'with all the talk there's been about Mr Pockett's treasure and the newspapers coming down to take his photograph, I daresay we shall get more holiday makers than ever before this season. There's always a bright side to everything—that's what I say.'

A remark which made Alan's mouth open so violently that he felt his jaw click.

'By the by,' the fair-haired lady went on, 'I'm glad to have a chance to have a word with you, Mrs Craig. Those cakes you made for the Bring and Buy were really delicious, my two residents brought some back to the hotel and we all had a little sample. Chef never makes cakes half as nice and it suddenly occurred to me that perhaps you might supply a regular order. If you can manage it that is?'

'I'm sure I could,' said Mrs Craig and she put her handkerchief away, much to Lorna's relief and smiled.

Alan and Johnny both remembered the Djinn at the same moment and at a nod from his brother, Johnny slid through the crowds and pulled the Djinn out of his hiding place and set off down the road with him as fast as he could go. He was not a moment too soon, for at that second the Vicar appeared with Mr Grant and said:

'Most gratifying, most. An altogether delightful speech, I wonder if I might use some of the things you said in my next sermon? There's been a lot of bad feeling in the town since old Pockett's good fortune, but I really believe that things will start to improve from now on. Tell me, Mr Grant, why did you choose Sandstone for your holiday, did you know it of old?'

'I don't believe I've ever been here before,' Mr Grant said thoughtfully, 'and yet in a strange way it all seems very familiar to me. It was as though I did visit it when I was a boy, but that's quite impossible as I was brought up in an orphanage in Glasgow. I wish I understood why one has these odd fancies.'

'I wish we had a larger hall,' said the Vicar, wiping his hot face.

'I think that might be arranged,' Mr Grant said, 'I feel I owe you something for all the upset there's been over this redevelopment plan. It was purely a slip up at Head Office.' He turned to smile at the Craigs and then, noticing the fair-haired lady he went on, 'I must apologise for going off at such short notice. Some sort of brainstorm I suppose.'

'Dear, dear,' said the fair-haired lady. 'Well I must say you look much, much better for it, brainstorm or not. Now then,' and she smiled at all of them, even Alan and Lorna, 'why don't you all come back to the hotel with me? We'll have a nice cup of tea. On the house.'

Mrs Craig and the Vicar and Mr Grant accepted the invitation and Mr Blofelt, who looked extremely unwell, said he'd go back with them but wouldn't have any tea as he rather wanted to have a lie down. Mr Antrobus declined too as he wanted to have a word with Alan and Lorna.

'Some other time then,' the fair-haired lady said and then she added softly so that only Alan and Lorna could hear, 'I'm sorry if I was a bit short-tempered with you. I don't know what came over me. You will come and see me one day won't you?'

'Yes thank you,' said Lorna in a whisper, but Alan was still too surprised to speak. They followed Mr Antrobus to his house feeling bewildered and rather flat now that all the excitement was over.

'It's about that friend of yours, Mr Chinn,' said Mr Antrobus, starting to search through all his pockets for his key, 'do you think he'd be willing to help me do some research on my ancestor Horatio? Funny, you know, he seems to have a fund of information about the chap, almost as though he knew him personally. Drat, where is the thing?'

'Under the mat,' said Lorna handing him the key.

'I'm sure he'd help if he could,' Alan said, thinking very fast, 'but you see he wants to get back to Arabia and he hasn't got any money so...'

'Bless you boy, I'm offering him a job,' said Mr Antrobus. 'Now who's this? If it's anything to do with the newspapers or television I'm out.'

A black car drew up alongside them just as Mr Antrobus started to fade backwards into his house. A man got out and came up to them, lifting his hat politely.

'Wonder if you could help us, sir?' he said. 'We're looking for a Mr Pockett, Ephraim Pockett.'

'He's outside the Smugglers' Rest having his photograph taken,' said Lorna. 'It's for the newspapers you know because of his treasure.'

'Is that so?' said the man and he smiled in a rather odd way. 'Thank you very much.'

'Straight down the road and turn left at the first corner,' said Alan helpfully. 'But if you want to photograph him, it'll cost you a shilling.'

'Is that so,' the man said again and this time both he and his companion laughed as though they'd heard a good joke and the car drove off.

'Wonder what that was all about,' said Mr Antrobus. 'Now then about Mr Chinn, do you know where he's staying?'

'Oh about,' said Alan vaguely. 'But we see him every day. We could always give him a message.'

'Good,' said Mr Antrobus filling the kettle, 'then here's what I'd like you tell him. I intend to write a book about Horatio Antrobus and I want him to help me with it and come with me to Arabia, so that I can reconstruct his travels there. Do you think he'd agree?'

'Oh yes,' said Lorna, throwing her arms round Mr Antrobus and hugging him tightly.

'I think he might,' said Alan, smiling from ear to ear.

14. *Johnny Makes a Wish*

It was a beautiful morning, just like a midsummer's day instead of an April one. The sky was a milky blue, the first lambs were jumping round the marsh as though they had springs on their feet and the garden round the Water Tower was speckled with golden celandines.

Mrs Craig had gone to deliver her first batch of cakes to the hotel and Lorna had seized the opportunity at long last to iron the Djinn's clothes for him. She was doing it very carefully and had her tongue caught between her teeth.

'We're going to miss you,' Alan said truthfully, looking at the Djinn who was wrapped in an eiderdown with a tea-cosy on his head. He was sitting cross-legged on the kitchen table humming softly to himself and his cheeks were flushed pale green with happiness. He had quite lost the sallow look which four hundred years under the sea had given him.

'And I shall miss you too,' the Djinn said. 'Ah for the camel train at dusk, the sweet oasis, the gurgle of spring water.'

'It may have changed a bit you know,' Alan said, 'I mean they have oilfields and aeroplanes and Cadillacs in Arabia these days.'

'It will still be the same out in the desert,' the Djinn said dreamily. 'The desert *never* changes. It is like the sea,' and he shuddered slightly.

'Where's Johnny?' asked Lorna, pushing her wrist across her face. It really was a very warm day.

'He went to see the television people packing up all their gear after last night's programme,' said Alan, 'and when that was over he was going to find out if Mr Pockett had been arrested and sent to prison.'

'They won't *really* put him in prison will they?' Lorna asked.

'No,' said the Djinn. 'My friend Mr Antrobus says that the aged and venerable Mr Pockett merely made a mistake. He was not to know that hidden treasures had to be declared to the police.'

'I bet,' Alan said to himself.

'Won't they let him keep any of the coins?' Lorna asked, gingerly touching the iron with one finger.

'Mr Antrobus fears not,' replied the Djinn. 'It seems hard, but it's probably all for the best. Money has a way of interfering with magic, there's always trouble in the end. I remember the time when a certain rich merchant...'

'He must be furious,' said Lorna. 'There, that's the trousers done,' and she held them up to show him. The Djinn bowed low and put his hands together.

'It's stopped everybody else rushing down to the beach and digging anyway,' said Alan, 'and it's not too bad really because he isn't going to get turned out of his house and Miss Pockett told me that her father was going to charge the tourists half-a-crown to take his photographs this summer. He says he's worth it because he's had his picture in the papers. He's going to charge for his autograph too.'

'So all is well,' said the Djinn. He cleared his throat. 'There is something which I should have told you, but alas I was too vain and...'

'There's your shirt,' Lorna said, 'you'd better hurry up and change. Mr Antrobus will be here in the taxi quite soon.'

The Djinn took the clothes and climbed into the broom cupboard to change. His voice, rather muffled, came through the door.

'You have never wished for yourselves,' he said, 'only for the good of your mother or for others. Is there no last service I can perform for you? It is customary.'

'Well I can't think...' said Lorna putting away the iron. 'Oh yes, there is one thing.'

'Come,' said the Djinn, 'and whisper it to me through the key-hole.'

Alan helped himself to one of the cakes which had been left over from the batch his mother had baked earlier and frowned. What could he wish for? What was there that he really wanted? He couldn't think of anything because the Water Tower was safe and the Wicked Landlord had turned into unfrightening Mr Grant and his mother was happy.

'Your turn,' said Lorna returning from the keyhole.

Alan went across very slowly and whispered too and even as he did so there was the sound of a taxi outside. The Djinn threw open the door and stood there looking quite completely different from the first time they had seen him. He seemed larger and much more sure of himself, but the greatest difference of all was his happy, confident smile.

'Oh I *am* sorry you're going,' Lorna said again.

'It is written in the stars,' the Djinn said, taking her hand and bowing over it. 'I shall never forget you. As I ride on the whirlwind through the desert I shall think of you often. As the pale moon rises over...'

'Morning,' said Mr Antrobus appearing in the doorway. 'My word you *do* look splendid Mr Chinn. National dress I suppose? Quite puts us in the shade.'

'You're sure you'll be all right,' said Lorna, smoothing out a tiny wrinkle in the Djinn's shirt.

'I will now,' said the Djinn, with a sidelong glance at Alan who looked rather embarrassed. He said quickly.

'We did enjoy the programme last night Mr. Antrobus We went over to the hotel to watch it. We clapped at the end.'

'It was awful, dreadful, horrible,' said Mr Antrobus, shuddering at the memory. 'They put *powder* on my head to stop it shining. I haven't the least idea what I said either. I felt a great *loon.*'

'It was super, honestly,' Lorna comforted him.

'Good of you to say so. That television fellow seems very taken with this place—even though he did spend a day digging and all for nothing—where was I? Oh yes, he's going to do another programme here, all about Sandstone and my house and the Water Tower and old Pockett. He wanted someone to act as a sort of guide and I suggested you. Knew you wanted to be on the television. Can't think why.'

'Me?' said Lorna, 'me on television. Oh Mr Antrobus!'

'It was what she wished wasn't it?' Alan whispered to the Djinn who nodded and then said:

'It was most thoughtful and considerate of you to wish as you did, oh Alan.'

'That's all right,' Alan said gruffly, 'couldn't have you granting wishes all along the journey after all. So I had to wish that you couldn't give wishes till you got back to the desert. I couldn't think of anything I wanted you see.'

'You are indeed fortunate,' said the Djinn softly, 'more fortunate than perhaps you realise. However, I believe that just for once I can break a rule...' And he shut his eyes and shivered and at the same moment the taxi driver appeared in the doorway with his arms clasped round a large packing case.

'Mr Antrobus, sir,' he said, 'this is where you wanted it, isn't it?'

'Bless my soul,' said Mr Antrobus, hitting his forehead, 'it's not like *me* to forget something. It's my television set. I never did like the thing and as I'm going away in any case I thought you might as well use it. Keep it from going rusty.'

'Thank you,' said Alan, 'thank you very much.' And he looked from Mr Antrobus to the Djinn who was smiling in an off-hand manner.

'Put it down there,' said Mr Antrobus to the taxi driver. 'Well we must be off. Are you ready Mr Chinn?'

'Yes Mr Antrobus,' said the Djinn holding the door open for him. They all trooped out into the garden and the Djinn fell back and grasped Alan's arm, saying in a low voice, 'There is something that I must tell. I am not a Djinn, although when I return to my native land and tell the Mighty One of what I have done, I believe I shall be promoted.'

'Not a Djinn!' Alan said blankly. 'But, but, but...'

'Merely a humble genii. I couldn't help boasting and I am deeply ashamed. That is why I could not let you see me without my turban. I have only a small pigtail not a six foot one as all real Djinns do. I thought you would guess if you saw it.'

'Well I wouldn't,' Alan said honestly. 'Don't worry, I won't tell the others and I'm sure they will make you a Djinn as soon as you get home. You deserve it.'

'Salaams,' the Djinn-Genii put his hands together and bowed low three times, 'Salaams, oh master.'

'I'm sorry Johnny isn't here to say goodbye,' said Lorna, opening the taxi door.

'We spoke earlier. He told me how he strongly disliked saying goodbye to a friend. Farewell.' The Djinn-Genii wiped a pale green tear off his cheek with one sleeve and the last glimpse they had of him was of one green hand waving violently from the back window of the taxi.

'I really shall miss him,' said Lorna, sniffing in her

turn, 'I do wish...' and then she stopped from force of habit and looked at Alan and they both burst out laughing.

'I wished I could be on television you know,' Lorna said, 'I wonder what Johnny—*Oh!*'

Brother and sister stared at each other for one horrified moment and then they both ran out of the garden gate and up to the top of the shingle bank. The sea was quite a long way out, glittering and glinting in the sunlight and making the sands dazzle with light too. And there squatting beside a rock pool and surrounded by seagulls was one small figure with a bucket.

'What could he have wished? Oh what could he have wished?' gasped Lorna as she slid down the bank after Alan.

But Alan was already sprinting across the sand towards his brother. The seagulls took to their wings and flew squawking up into the warm blue sky, but Johnny didn't even bother to look up as Alan reached him. He was intent on digging something carefully out of the deep rock pool.

'Has he gone?' Johnny asked.

'Yes.'

'I said goodbye after breakfast,' said Johnny, dipping his hands deeper into the clear water. 'I don't like friends going away so I didn't want to see it. He was my very particular *esteemed* friend.'

'He granted you a wish didn't he?' Alan asked, trying to sound not very interested. Johnny nodded. 'What?' Alan said, holding his breath and putting up one hand to keep Lorna quiet as she came puffing up to them.

'We're not supposed to tell,' Johnny said.

'We weren't supposed to ask *him*,' Alan said, just

managing to keep his impatience under control. 'Go on, what did you wish?'

Johnny knelt back on his heels and squinted up at them.

'I wished to find a mermaid,' he said solemnly.

'JOHNNY YOU DIDN'T!' Lorna and Alan said in the same breath.

Johnny sat looking up at them and then he turned to watch the sparkling sea and the white circling gulls and finally he turned his attention back to the deep, mysterious pool.

' 'Course I didn't,' he said, 'I wished for a nice day so as I could look for crabs. I think I've got one too. Give us the bucket.'

STAY ON

INVESTIGATING UFOs 25p

Larry Kettelkamp

0 426 10006 9 **A Target Mystery**

The full, dramatic story of unidentified flying objects or 'Flying Saucers' as they are commonly called. Visitors from other planets? Optical illusions? Or practical jokes? With the help of INVESTIGATING UFOs you can decide for yourself and even join one of the 20 or more UFO clubs in the United Kingdom. *Fully illustrated with photographs and drawings.*

THE STORY OF THE LOCH NESS MONSTER 25p

Tim Dinsdale

0 426 10073 5 **A Target Mystery**

What mysterious entity lurks beneath the 1000 ft. deep, sinister-looking waters of Loch Ness in the Highlands of Scotland? Since the 1930s, men have sought the answer to this question. The author, a full-time, professional monster-hunter, tells you the history of the search for 'Nessie', and her cousin 'Morag', the monster of Loch Morar, and of the latest discoveries made with scientific equipment. *Fully illustrated with maps, photographs, and drawings.*

SMALL CREATURES IN MY BACK GARDEN 25p

Christopher Reynolds

0 426 10049 2

Have you a back garden or even a yard or some-such place that you can visit regularly? There are many tiny creatures that you are likely to find there besides the more familiar snails, ants and worms. . . . And with the simplest equipment, mostly home-made, the author shows you how to create new worlds of interest and delight. *Illustrated.*

ROCKET TO FAME 25p

John Rowland

0 426 10401 3

Here is the dramatic story of the man who was architect of Britain's world-famous railway system—George Stephenson, whose famous 'Rocket' won the great locomotive competition of 1829—the story of a genius who grasped hold of his destiny with both hands and within the space of a few years transformed the life of a nation! *Illustrated.*